THE DECLINE OF AN ENGLISH VILLAGE

ROBIN PAGE

Foreword by Zac Goldsmith

Illustrated by Roger Phillippo

BIRD'S FARM BOOKS

By the Same Author
The Benefits Racket
Down Among the Dossers
The Decline of an English Village
The Hunter and the Hunted
Weather-forecasting the Country Way
Cures and Remedies the Country Way
Animal Cures the Country Way
Weeds the Country Way
The Journal of a Country Parish
Journeys into Britain
The Country Way of Love
The Wildlife of the Royal Estates
A Fox's Tale
The Fox and the Orchid
Dust in a Dark Continent (Africa)
Gardening the Country Way
A Peasant's Diary
Gone to the Dogs
Vocal Yokel
Carry on Farming
The Hunting Gene
One Man Went to Mow
The Great British Butterfly Safari

Children's Books
How the Fox got its Pointed Nose
How the Heron got Long Legs
Why the Rabbit Stamps its Foot
How the Hedgehog got its Prickles
Why the Reindeer has a Velvet Nose

Published by Bird's Farm Books, Barton, Cambridgeshire CB3 7AG
www.crtbarton.com
Distributed by Merlin Unwin Books, 7 Corve Street, Ludlow, Shropshire

First published in 1974 by Davis-Poynter Ltd
Copyright © 2004 30th Anniversary Edition

ISBN 0 905232 23 2

Designed by Jim Reader
Design and production in association with Book Production Consultants plc,
25–27 High Street, Chesterton, Cambridge CB4 1ND
www.bpccam.co.uk

Printed and bound in Great Britain by The Burlington Press, Foxton, Cambridge

Contents

———

The Thirtieth Anniversary Edition

of

The Decline of an English Village

———

This new edition of *The Decline of an English Village* marks the 30th anniversary of the original publication in 1974. Since that time, there have been thirty years of unremitting change in the countryside as a whole – as well as in my particular English village, where I was born and where I still live. Thirty years of writing – thirty years of living – gone – vanished – and nothing I have written, thought or attempted has altered or slowed the pace of change. I have changed only one word of the original volume – for some reason 'beech' trees near the village school became 'elms'.

The book describes what I saw and felt as a young villager – seeing change as rapid as it had been since the start of recorded history. I have simply added a new epilogue, showing that time has removed my innocence and replaced it with a contempt for those who rule, and misrule, us.

My village is quite unremarkable – that is why it is important – for its fate can be seen in countless other villages up and down the country. Under the guise of 'progress' a whole way of life is disappearing and has disappeared. New values and new aspirations are replacing the old: something of value, of culture, of reality is being lost – for what?

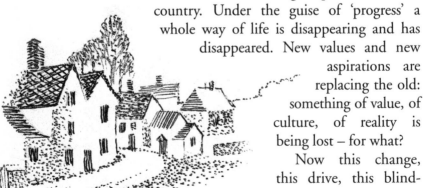

Now this change, this drive, this blindness is spreading further

– to Europe and the continents beyond – it is a story of rural culture disappearing, of people being dispossessed, and of communities losing their land, their beliefs, their traditions – losing themselves.

This version has been embellished with the sketches of Roger Phillippo – another of that diminishing band who feel the loss and so is regarded, by and large, as an eccentric. The 21st century is no place for eccentrics – it is new, brave and looking forward – Brave New World. We've heard it all before: reality shows that we are losing our understanding of nature, of community, of the seasons, of the way we grow our food. We are becoming detached from the things that sustain us, improve us and give us added quality to our lives. Semi-detached people in a world that we understand and value less and less; we are becoming rootless, losing both our culture and our identity.

I hope that this edition of *The Decline of an English Village* will encourage people to ask three simple questions: What are we doing? Where are we going? Why?

Robin Page
Cambridgeshire 2004

Foreword

by Zac Goldsmith

———

I had the privilege after leaving school of being able to tour parts of Asia, New Zealand and Central America. On my travels I bore witness to countless obvious injustices: the traditional culture of Ladakh succumbing to the brutality of 'development'; whole communities in northern India being uprooted to make way for a giant dam; indigenous communities of southern Mexico deprived of their dignity, existing in fifth-rate urban squalor.

Like most people exposed to these tragedies, I was angry and depressed. But it all seemed so distant from everything I knew, until someone gave me a copy of Robin Page's *The Decline of an English Village*. Reading it changed my view of the world. Suddenly it became obvious that the forces behind that mindless destruction are at work in my country too, the only difference being that they have been at work here for much longer. Perhaps that is why the majority of us simply adjust to these trends rather than fight them as we should. Perhaps that is why we accept decline as if it were somehow evolutionary.

Needless to say, it's not evolutionary. Rural decline is the consequence of bad, often corrupt decisions born of an unholy marriage between politics and vastly over-sized businesses. When confronted with the effects of those bad decisions, our leaders merely interpret them in such a way as to legitimise further bad decisions.

As a result our rural communities are being gutted. At the turn of the 21st century, only half of Britain's parishes boasted a shop, farm incomes had plummeted to an average of £10,000 and farmers were committing suicide at a rate of one each week. Rural Britain is dying, like the communities of southern Mexico, like the cultures of northern India.

Faced with all this, the experts appeal to abstract economic principles which they regard with far greater deference than they do real people. If farmers are going out of business, they say, it is because they are 'uneconomic'. But to be 'economic' in today's global food economy requires political access, disproportionate subsidies, and an ability to make the relentless costs of intensive agriculture – pesticides, erosion, emissions, cancer – vanish from the price tags of artificially 'cheap' food. Facilities, in other words, that could not be further from the grasp of an ordinary farmer. Unsurprisingly there is a rural crisis in virtually every region on Earth.

Today's engineers of 'progress' are pushing us blindfold from a past they refuse to acknowledge towards a future that they cannot define. There are no realistic goals, and therefore no means by which we may judge its course. Brave New World developments are sprung on our countryside – but like the crowds assembled to view the naked Emperor's new clothes, too few of us are prepared to say what is true; that transforming rural communities into vacuous commuter zones, their inhabitants to mere economic units, does not represent 'progress'. It represents death.

Working communities, of the sort Robin Page describes in this beautiful book, take generations to build but only a few years to destroy. They are vital threads in the fabric of British life, and fulfil priceless social, ecological and economic functions. Common sense dictates that we should cherish and nurture them.

This is a story of the tragic unravelling of one such community at the hands of a new elite whose rejection of anything that fails to conform to its sanitised urban world is pursued with all the vehemence of a Jihad.

It's hard to read *The Decline of an English Village* without developing a deep sense of longing for a life that no amount of material advantage can deliver. For the first time in our history as a species, we have been stripped of our context, like a snail stripped of its shell. We may not be able to go back to the society Robin Page describes, but we can use his often amusing and always moving tale as a beacon by which to rebuild this country on sane principles.

Introduction

This book is not meant to be an autobiography, although much of it concerns my childhood, nor is it a scholarly thesis, it is simply an attempt to describe the gradual death of a village community; a death that has taken many years to accomplish, and which is now almost complete.

It spans a period of time from the end of the Second World War until almost the present day, and shows how the whole tenor of country life has changed and is changing. During the 1940s, the scene was virtually as it had been for generations, apart from one or two mechanical innovations, with men working on the land, boys following in their fathers' footsteps, and women busying themselves with the home and family.

Characters who had been moulded by the hardness of life, the machinations of money making, or the infidelity of the elements, lived and worked together in the village to form a real community. It was not unique, as similar ones could be found throughout the country, but sadly little of it now remains.

Sex was taught to the young by sparrows performing acts of passion on the pea sticks; the three 'Rs', by the village school mistress; and life in general was dictated by the seasons of the year and the 'Will of God'.

Today, evidence of progress has changed the village almost beyond recognition. The land is no longer the centre of life, on which men have to co-operate or compete with nature for survival, it is merely an economic commodity to be bought or sold.

Children now learn about sex from school manuals, men and women commute daily into towns for employment, the seasons of the year are unimportant and life is dictated entirely by economic considerations. Materially, all have benefited, but at the same time the quality of life has been impoverished. God has taken a holiday.

The occurrences in this book are not in chronological order, and season does not follow season, for memories of a village childhood are timeless. Events have been retained in my mind as a series of images, and these, sometimes blurred by the passage of time and refreshed by the memories of others, I have endeavoured to record. They show, I hope, a way of life that is rapidly dying; a change from a simple and palpable past, to an ephemeral present and an impersonal synthetic future. A change that has affected not only the society in which we live, but also our priorities, and ourselves.

Robin Page
Cambridgeshire 1974

CHAPTER 1

Home and Farm

———

As the Second World War moved towards its grand finale, so the situation on mainland Europe grew ever more bloody. Mobile and efficient means of inflicting death were being used with greater accuracy and skill, and still more sophisticated methods of destruction were being put into production. It was a time of horror, havoc and change.

The atmosphere in rural England, however, made a complete contrast, and apart from the blackouts and the patriotic duties of 'Dad's Army', life went on untroubled and at the same pace as it had for generations. In fact the only real difference between war and peace was that financially conditions were much better while hostilities lasted; for it was, and still is, a belief held by the farming community, both man and master, that 'they' only care about farming during a war – a view that is not entirely without foundation.

Farms were still a mixture of small fields and copses, of arable and pastoral, of horse power and manual labour. The technical advances that had been made to mete out death had not yet been translated into new ways of relieving the burden of work and combating the elements.

It was on a typical farm in south-west Cambridgeshire that I was born in 1943; the result of a union between a butcher turned farmer and a farmer's daughter turned teacher. I was delivered blue and crying; having tried to enter the world side-ways; not in a farmhouse, but in a small semi-detached cottage, where I joined a sister and a brother.

Our water was pumped by hand, outside the scullery window, and the bucket lavatory was across a small concrete path, a journey which to a small boy on a raw winter's night was both frightening and cold. The garden was like most country gardens at that time, with daisies flowering in the lawn and a vegetable patch near the back door where marrows seemed to swell to gargantuan proportions. Silver birch, apple and plum trees grew in abundance, as well as a caterpillar tree that every summer attracted hordes of black and red hairy caterpillars. Hens scrapped busily at the bottom of the garden, where large elms stood like guardians of the peace.

The house was a happy place, the natural projection of a romance that had started when my Mother was twelve and my Father thirteen. The exchange of love letters, sweets and stolen kisses, had grown into the setting up of a home and the rearing of a family. Mother, at four feet eleven and three-quarter inches, had energy far in excess of her height and all day long she bustled here and there, cooking, sweeping, collecting eggs, singing hymns, and humming. Fine old country smells wafted through the house, chutney, jams, pies and sometimes home-made bread, and not a scrap of food was wasted. During her childhood Mother had experienced hard times; fatherless at the age of ten, she had been brought up to count the pennies. Every spring while at school she had taken daffodils into Cambridge to sell for extra money and had even sold bunches of snowdrops at school. Because of this she had a real fear of poverty, but fortunately hard times were past and all was well.

God had been good to her and now her simple faith dictated that she should show her gratitude by working for him during her mortal life. Consequently, from dawn to dusk she would effervesce with an uplifting religious zeal, looking after the home, doing odd jobs on the farm, taking meals to neighbours who were old or sick, and comforting those in distress. She was invariably in a rush, but despite her sedulity, she always made time for her children as we were the ones who would carry on her good work after she had departed this life; departed, she believed and hoped, to a world full of song and love, where white clad figures would teach her to play the harp.

The order of life would sometimes be disrupted by a dispute or a disaster, but she could always cope. Scuffles would develop over the possession of a military pedal-car which had a large American star emblazoned on its bonnet and the guilty party would be sent with slapped and stinging legs to sit on a chair. Disasters were different and were always treated with understanding and sympathy. The pump, to me, was always a fascination, the curved dripping spout, the handle on which I could swing, and the water, clear and cool, appearing iridescent as it fell through sunlight to be caught in mouthfuls and spat out again in miniature fountains of liquid ice. Fascinating, that was,

3

until one morning, without warning, a bumble bee fell dead and soggy from the spout. It had obviously been lurking there for me, or had been sucked up from the very centre of the earth, and screaming, I fled into the house; sure enough Mother reassured me and without a great deal of difficulty managed to keep my panic at bay.

Brother John also had a memorable moment of terrifying confrontation, with a wasp. Father's hands were hard and horny from physical labour, and during the summer he would demonstrate this by crushing wasps with his thumb. The victim, dead and quivering, would then automatically plunge its sting into his skin. Feeling nothing he would lift his prey aloft, hanging by its sting from his thumb. One morning John crept up on a wasp that was battering itself on a window pane, and, to show his manhood, he dealt out a similar death. It worked, but so too did the sting, and he stood screaming as he held up his prize.

Disruption of a different kind came shortly after the war in the form of a television set. It had a nine-inch screen and had been bought for my paternal grandmother who lay bedridden with arthritis; but she, a quiet, philosophical woman, refused to watch it. Consequently it came to us, and we had the dubious distinction of being the first family in the village with 'a telly'. To some it was a miracle of communication, to others it was the work of the 'very Devil himself', but whatever it was we enjoyed it, and every so often the house would fill up with people wanting to see the Cup Final, the Boat Race or Trooping the Colour.

Life became one continuous adventure; a tank, home from the war, turned round in the road

4

outside the house, and every day gave some fresh experience or heralded the awakening of a new awareness. Summer mornings wet with dew, shafts of orange sunlight drifting through the gossamer threads of a spider's web; a row of dead and headless hens after a visit from a fox; the visit of the doctor after Father had put a garden fork through his foot; and the old lady next door, her wrinkled, crumbling face balanced on the top of a long black dress and surrounded by lace, all contributed to an ever changing tapestry of life.

But the greatest adventure of all was a visit to the farm just along the road. There were animals to watch or chase, puddles in which to splash or fall, and if we were lucky we would get a ride in grand-father's pony and trap. Grandfather, a successful businessman, had moved into the farm several years before after starting out in life as a shepherd boy, and then becoming a butcher. In his early days he had soon realised how money was made, but also saw that it was more sensible to make money for himself rather than for an employer. His modestly started butchery enterprise had quickly grown into a minia-ture meat empire, with a factory, delivery vans and several shops; 'Page's sausages' became a household name locally, and were eaten in the humblest working class homes as well as at the lavish banqueting tables of the colleges.

It came as a surprise to me one day to learn that we were to move into the farmhouse. Grandfather had apparently gone off 'to be with Jesus' and wouldn't be coming back, and the whole family had to move to take his place. A trailer was loaded up with furniture, tables, beds and chairs, perched precariously on top of each other, and a spluttering Fordson Major tractor pulled us in style to our new home.

The farmhouse was old, built about 1470, covered with thatch and full of rooms with low ceilings. An old lady in the village could remember visiting it at the turn of the century when there had been no upstairs windows and the occupants had gone to bed through a hole in the living room ceiling, bed being a pile of straw on the floor. Up in the roof the wooden beams were stained with soot, from a time when there had been no chimney, and the whole house felt as if it had grown up out of the ground on which it stood.

It was a fine house, giving security and shelter at times, and at others providing mystery and discomfort. On still, dark nights the beams would heave and send out long low groans and there was said to be a large open fireplace and an old bread oven sealed up in one of the walls. During hot weather the rooms would remain pleasantly cool, but during cold, they would freeze and the wind would seemingly blow straight through the walls. Log fires would burn vigorously in the grates, throwing out considerable heat when not really needed, and then, when required, they would smoulder and die, sometimes filling the rooms with choking clouds of smoke. It soon acquired the atmosphere of the old cottage, however, and with a coke-burning Aga in the kitchen, the pedal-car parked under the living room table and a newer even larger garden, it was quickly established as home.

Father was now a farmer in his own right. He had always wanted to be one, but nobody had taken him seriously and he had trained for the life-long task of cutting up carcasses and counting money. He had also wanted to become a veterinary surgeon, but this, too, was considered an unworthy ambition for someone with business at his feet and in his blood. At school he had studied for business, in readiness for his rightful place in the family firm; he had learnt book-keeping and accountancy and had gone through the butchery trade from bottom to top. He had scrubbed benches, made sausages, killed pigs, boned gammon and made brawn. He had then got married and announced that he intended to become a farmer. He had lived on the farm as a boy, and as Mother's roots went back into the land for several generations, spreading out into the Fens, the idea appealed to both of them. It was not seen as a means of making money, but more as a way of life; a part of the eternal struggle for survival, which possessed far more dignity than selling mutton chops over a counter, or sitting in a director's chair.

In wanting him to become a butcher, his parents had failed to take into consideration that their marriage, (my grand-father's second, as his first wife had died), linked together two most extraordinary and independent families. Among their ranks had been abstainers and brewers, radical free-thinkers and blue-nosed Tories, churchmen and atheists, labourers and layabouts, and Father had inherited idiosyncrasies from nearly all of them. The fact that he should insist on becoming a farmer against all their wishes was therefore not really in the least bit surprising.

He was a strange but likeable mixture of diligence and dilatoriness, tolerance and turbulence, wisdom and wilfulness. He castigated his brother for being a member of the Conservative Party, but at the same time announced that it was impossible to be both a Christian and a Socialist. He referred to freemasons as 'the forty thieves' and condemned profit; yet at the same time he joined the Country Landowners Association and lived by selling his milk, eggs, and corn for as much as he could get. He admired Oliver Cromwell but insisted that you could not mix religion and politics, and his Christian philosophy was in a constant state of flux, leaping the chasm from liberalism to fundamentalism and vice versa with amazing regularity and ease.

But to me, as a child, his contradictions went unnoticed; he was my Father, a man respected, feared and admired. He taught me how to feed young calves, collect eggs without being pecked by broody hens, how to play cricket and bowl 'spinners', how to receive a new baby sister into the family, and by his example he showed me how to respect life. During times of disease or maternity he would sit for hours with the animals, helping, healing, and encouraging, and he would demonstrate patience and understanding to them that he would not give to men. In fact his whole mode of living was quite remarkable, for in effect he had virtually opted out of conventional society. He seldom went into Cambridge, he rarely had money in his pocket, appearance and prestige concerned him not at all, and because of this, as I grew older I ceased to see him as a father-figure, but as a friend.

Life on the land was hard, requiring patience, resourcefulness and brute force. During a hot dry summer the thick grey boulder clay, which seemed to descend to unfathomable depths, would set as solid as rock, its adamantine crust blunting implements, wearing out horseshoes and causing frustration and despair. If ploughed late it would dry out, forming countless clods of varying sizes from marbles to footballs, and elsewhere it would crack, the heat from the sun drawing out the moisture, leaving the crops struggling for survival. In contrast, winter would show the full fickleness of its nature and it would become a squelching, glutinous mass, turning the farmyard into a sea of mud and making land work impossible; work was confined to ditching or hedging with hands numb with cold, cutting kale with clothing soaked by the chilling leaf-held water, repairing buildings, or shovelling out 'muck' from the cowshed and the stable.

Dolly and Diamond were housed in the stable; two fine cart-horses, one the colour of burnt sienna, the other a dark chestnut. They were said to be a Clydesdale and a Shire, but time and hot blood had allowed other strains to creep in. Their confidence, bearing and strength, a living tribute to their ancestry, made them not only able and willing workers, but also valuable companions in the never-ending struggle with the elements. But, sadly, as they stood at their manger, snorting and stamping, proud and content, they were unaware of the significance of the blue tractor standing silently in the shed nearby. It needed no care when not working, its hunger was for toil not sustenance, it was strong, adaptable, and reliable. The adoption of the Fordson Major marked the beginning, and the end, of an era.

Because of the tractor Dolly soon left, sold to a dealer, who in turn sold her again, probably to a factory in Melton Mowbray where she would disappear inside tins of catfood, or to be exported to Belgium, destined for a butcher's shop in Bruges. When I was eight, another lorry arrived, this time for Diamond, and she too was loaded up and whisked away. It was a miserable day on the farm. Two tractors now stood in the shed and the stable was empty, save for memories and the smell of the past. I would have no more rides on that broad brown back, clinging with trusting arms to her shaggy greying mane, and she would pull no more cart loads of water along the road for the cows as they grazed languorously in a nearby meadow. The harsh facts of farming life meant that she had to go. She had worked willingly and well, but her coat was losing its lustre, her muscles were tiring and her reactions were slowing. The faithful horse that had toiled for hours in the fields, shifting tons of corn and earth, was finished, and her large mournful eyes seemed to know this. Father could not hide the sense of betrayal he felt in sending his helper to the knacker's yard; a helpmeet who had aided him in bad times and good, and whose crime was that of old age. Apart from her age she had only one minor failing; an almost uncanny sense of time. Regardless of her task, whether she was hoeing, ploughing or drilling, as soon as it was time to stop, her time, not her master's, she would turn at right angles and head for home. Now she would be returning home no more.

Father felt that same sense of betrayal and guilt when he sent cows to market to be sold for slaughter. For ten or twelve years he would feed them and house them, in winter mixing their food with a shovel on the floor of the barn, turning over and stirring the multi-coloured mound of different meals like a builder mixing cement, and in return they would give him milk and every year deliver him a new calf. Then, as soon as their yield dropped or they became barren, they were sold off and killed. The economic facts of life did not allow for sentiment, and the saddest sound on the farm was that of the cattle lorry as it revved up and moved off to Cambridge.

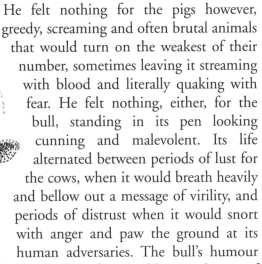

He felt nothing for the pigs however, greedy, screaming and often brutal animals that would turn on the weakest of their number, sometimes leaving it streaming with blood and literally quaking with fear. He felt nothing, either, for the bull, standing in its pen looking cunning and malevolent. Its life alternated between periods of lust for the cows, when it would breath heavily and bellow out a message of virility, and periods of distrust when it would snort with anger and paw the ground at its human adversaries. The bull's humour was worsened by the fact that around the farm buildings and some of the fields, the animals were kept in by an electric fence; a thin strand of wire through which an electric current passed every second. We normally kept well away from it, hating every time we accidentally received a shock, but greatly enjoying the sight of an unsuspecting visitor taking hold of it. The bull disliked it, after allowing the chain from his nose to become entangled with it and then retreating backwards, only for another strand of wire to send a shock rushing up his tail.

The wire had hardly any effect on Father who would casually take hold of it, to check that it was not shorting, with no apparent discomfort. When moving the wire one morning, to allow the cows to get at some new grass, he was watched by several children, including an innocent boy from the High Street: 'Get hold of that end for me will you, Paul?' he asked. Paul picked it up with both hands; his eyes blinked in amazement, his mouth opened, and every time the current passed through him his whole body jolted. He was so surprised that he just stood there pulsating and bemused until Father told him to let go.

Every day, twice a day, the cows had to be milked, at first by hand, and then by a new milking machine that pulled and sucked, faster and more efficiently than the human hand. The churns had to be lugged and manhandled to the dairy and then to the roadside for collection, the pigs and hens had to be fed, and in addition the land had to be cultivated.

All this could not be done by one man alone and Father had two full-time workers to help him, and sometimes three. Jim and Percy were the regulars, one a countryman born and bred, the other a townsman who would have been more at home delivering milk or repairing pavements. It was Percy who was out of place on the land, for he was unacquainted with the laws of nature and could not understand the animals. Land work had been for him a stop-gap, taken up when jobs were difficult to come by, but he worked happily, if fitfully, and used such words as 'shite', the meanings of which we were supposed not to know.

Jim was completely different, a small, one-eyed, well-meaning countryman, who could read the condition of the land or the seasons of the year like others read a book. His father, grandmother and great-grandfather had all been tenants of the same farm and were

from that ancient yeoman stock which had formed the stable backbone of English society for generations. Men of resolution and reliance who had farmed and fought with a resilience and a determination that had made them an asset to any cause, and who, when Oliver Cromwell had represented Cambridge in Parliament, flocked to his banner to overthrow what they saw as injustice and tyranny. Jim had maintained that tradition, and in 1914 he, too, had responded to the call of duty and went to do battle in northern France. After just six months of active service he had returned home with honour, but also with a shrapnel wound in his right eye. He lost his eye, but gained a view of the French that time never changed and which, to him, the Second World War endorsed. The French were, he said, incapable of fighting, they were dirty and stupid, and France itself was not worth fighting for. 'If I had been a bloody Froggie,' he asserted, 'I'd have given the bugger to Jerry.' But he was proud of his sacrifice and even had a begrudging respect for 'the bloody squareheads', who were, he admitted, good soldiers and workers.

His father had been turned out of the rented farm when the land had changed hands, and as there had been no security of tenure Jim had not been able to become his own master. But this did not worry him unduly, and with a cigarette hanging from the corner of his mouth, and his one eye guiding him almost as well as two, he returned to the land as a worker, where he progressed with ease from horse to tractor, from harness to sparking plug, and became master of both.

Not surprisingly, after generations of independence and struggle, he was a Tory, who looked upon Socialism as a malignant cancer that ate into stability, freedom and self-respect. At the mention of certain politicians he would take off his cap, scratch his greying head in exasperation and recommend that the offending wretch be placed 'head first in a barrel of runny cow muck', or that a 'hedgehog skin should be wrapped around a pitchfork handle and stuffed up his bloody arse.'

Apart from his love of the land and his hatred of Socialism, his one abiding passion was cricket and he could talk for hours on the game, sounding like an encyclopaedia of all the great names of the past. He spoke of Hobbs and Sutcliffe, at Lord's and Parker's Piece, and recalled many memorable occasions on local village greens where amazing feats of batting had taken place, and where, on other occasions, teams had been skittled out for less than ten.

Charlie would occasionally arrive on his bicycle to work part-time. He was a signalman on the railway who rested while at work, and worked while he should have been resting at home. In his signal-box he could doze until roused by the warning bell, and at home he kept pigs, cultivated a large garden, as well as a plot of ground, and still had time to help out local farmers. At hay cart and harvest, others too would come for casual work or would be borrowed from neighbouring farms, so that the work could be speedily finished.

It was harvest time that we children liked the best, the sun always seemed to shine and there would be picnic teas 'down the harvest field'. There, Jim would drive the tractor, Father would sit on the binder, and the corn would be cut and tied into sheaves. The sheaves were carried, one under each arm, into groups of ten or twelve, and stood up on end into shocks. (In many other areas called 'stooks'.) Diamond and the tractor would then be used for carting; the tractor pulling its load easily and quickly, Diamond, towards her end, struggling, straining and sometimes slipping. Once roped on, the loads would lurch and sway as the trailers were pulled along the rough cart tracks, and we children would conceal our fear with laughter as we rode on top.

The men worked long hours to get the harvest home and would finish each day tired and hungry. But the smell of corn being cut, the creak of horse and harness, the feel of stubble on bare legs, the sun, rabbits being shot as they ran for cover, and Mother, forgetting briefly the evils of alcohol, buying quart bottles of cider, made it the best season of the year for us. The insects in the sandwiches, the horseflies droning menacingly in hungry search, and the fatigue of those working were of little consequence.

13

The other time of real excitement was in autumn or winter when the threshing tackle trundled up to thresh the stacks of corn. A large drum would arrive, a tractor, a baling machine, and a gang of brawny weathered men. They would set up the machinery, shouting and joking, taking life easily, and then, when all was ready, their torpor would be transformed into urgent industry. Two or three men would throw sheaves onto the drum. Another would cut the strings and feed the straw into the hungry machine and others would heave sacks of corn onto trailers or struggle with large bales of straw. The drum itself was a large throbbing hulk, covered with wheels, pulleys and belts, like a wild wooden animal, spewing dust and noise in all directions, and tethered to the tractor by a large drive belt. At one end the corn, threshed and separated from the chaff, flowed into comb sacks, which for wheat, when full, weighed eighteen stone, and at the other the straw fell into a baler which pounded out large wire-tied bales. ('Comb' – pronounced 'coomb', which for field beans was 19 stone, oats 12 stone, and barley 16 stone). The chaff was blown out of one side, and the 'ol' boy', usually a youth fresh from school, was given the task of keeping it in an orderly heap. It was the worst job of all for which nobody ever volunteered, and all day long he worked in a mantle of dust, the irritating husks getting into his hair, up his nose, in his eyes, inside his clothing and down his wellington boots.

For the men it was hot, sometimes heavy work, but for we children and the dogs it was a time of high adventure. As the stack got lower and the sheaves were moved, mice and rats would scamper in all directions. We would rush about in hot pursuit, brandishing large sticks, and each gnawing spoiler of corn would have to run a gauntlet of snapping jaws and flailing clubs. Weasels, too, would sometimes be disturbed, but they were not willing to accept death meekly and the dogs would often cry out in pain as razor sharp teeth sank into their flesh. Sometimes, in a fit of blind, furred fury a weasel would fling itself at the neck of a dog and stay hanging in a stream of its victim's blood, until killed mercilessly and brutally in a frenzy of anger and desperation.

Even those mice that did escape to the comparative safety of the surrounding stubble or plough land were still not safe, for the noise of threshing attracted other more noble predators; ones, who over the years had never been properly mastered by man and whose primeval wildness was still reflected in their savage brown eyes. The kestrels would hover in air on quivering wings, watching and waiting for life and movement. Then, without warning, they would fall like stones, the feathered projectiles of death, immediately crushing life away.

Each year it was the same threshing tackle that appeared on the farm and the men spent the whole of their winter travelling from farm to farm with the machines. One man, with a red face, a cap perched on the side of his head, and a smile on his face, was called Happy. Another, older man, with a wooden leg, looked like a pirate, and when out of earshot we called him Peg Leg. One day as the stack got lower, my brother and I, together with a crowd of other children, eagerly swarmed onto the stack in search of mice. Several times Happy and Peg Leg asked us civilly to get out of their way, and each time we soon returned, to try their patience to the limit. 'Go on, get off. That's the last time you'll be told,' the older man said finally. 'Why?' I replied, standing near him defiantly, 'It's not your stack – Peg Leg'. With that he swivelled round on his stump with surprising speed, catching me as he did so across the seat of my trousers with a stick. Happy's smile broke into a laugh, the other children retired discreetly and I fled homewards with hurt pride and a stinging seat. This proved beyond all doubt that Peg Leg was really a pirate and Father had to be told; yet all he said was: 'It serves you right,' and he thought it was funny too.

The other seasons of the year also brought their own distinctive features which dictated both work and play, and each one was welcomed in its turn. Shortly before corn harvest it was a time of plum picking, tree climbing and bark grazed knees. Boxes full of Early Rivers and Czars, with each plum bearing the bloomed finger prints of its picker, were piled onto a trailer and taken to the small railway station a mile away, to be loaded into trucks and sent to Liverpool and Manchester. It was a sleepy little station with just a few trains passing through each day and one occasionally stopping. Whenever we children were on the railway bridge and a train passed beneath, thundering, hissing, and belching out smoke, it was considered to be a great event. Some days, hours would be whiled away, dropping stones, or spitting at the rails from our lofty position, hoping that a train would come. The railway also served another purpose, for whenever the trains could be heard loud and clear in the village, it was a sure sign of rain, and just as accurate as a watery sun or a halo around the moon, and a far more reliable guide than the BBC weather forecast.

The orchard itself was old, only an acre in size, but full of large plum, apple and pear trees. In spring the undulating tree tops, florid and bright, appeared as fragrant peaks of freshly fallen snow, seemingly incandescent in the regenerative heat of the sun as it ascended higher in the sky towards its summer solstice. Gradually, as the blossom melted away, bees searched elsewhere for sweetness, and new green foliage gave movement to the wind. At this time it was a place of peace, dappled shade, goldfinches with moss lined nests, the occasional woodpecker probing and penetrating the flaking bark, and solitude. Later, as the leaves dulled and the fruit swelled, so the breeding pigs moved around their summer quarters with more enthusiasm. Sows would rootle in the grass for fallen fruit, their snouts sucking and searching noisily, and on finding a plum or apple they would smack their jaws together in a state of sensuous bliss. The boar, fat and indolent, would spend most of his time in the corner, lounging half-submerged in a black pool of stagnant, stinking mud; his appearance seemed to reflect his innermost thoughts. Regular visits were made to the orchard at this time to check the ripeness of the fruit, and green hard plums would be pelted at the pigs, or one another, until finally, when the plums were blue, or the apple pips rattled, pockets, as well as stomachs, would be filled to bursting point. The other major happening in the orchard appeared on November 5th. Then, a bonfire would blaze, and after fireworks had been lit and an effigy of Guy Fawkes burnt, any remaining apples would be picked and baked in the embers.

As soon as the harvest fields were emptied and the stacks of corn thatched (called ricks in some areas), a change could be detected not only on the land, but also in the air. Damp would linger on the grass until well into the day and mist would hang on the hedgerows until mid-morning. It was a time when swallows assembled, uneasy and voluble, on the telephone wires, and the trees and bushes seemed to absorb some of the rich, fiery opalescence of autumn sunsets.

Mushrooms larger than saucers could be found in the meadows, where the cows grazed away the last of their pasture, and everything seemed to be suspended in a state of indecision, between the life and vitality of summer and winter's quiescence.

It was at this time that Jim would don his old army great coat of faded khaki, and with his bag containing cold tea and sandwiches, his ancient twelve-bore shotgun, and the farmyard spaniel, Peter, at his heels, he would swing start the tractor and spend his days plough-ing. I would sometimes ride at his side as he ploughed a seemingly never ending furrow, while Peter watched patiently from the edge of the field, lying next to a bucket of grease and the gun. Lapwings would stand one-legged, looking bored or apprehensive, their wings glowing with a metallic green sheen, and seagulls would home in on the freshly turned soil and follow the plough, wheeling and stalling, climbing and diving, feeding and fighting, like thistledown in a whirlpool of wind.

At seed time, too, rides could be had during drilling; with Jim driving the tractor and Father on the drill behind, ensuring that the seed was properly sown. It seemed to me that the corn was put on far

too thickly, but Jim would say sagaciously: 'Four seeds you have to sow. One for the rook and one for the crow, one to die and one to grow.' Often, even as he said it, gangs of rooks would drift silently down, looking sleek and pompous. Once landed they would stroll about sedately and ponderously, like old men in black satin dinner jackets after a heavy lunch. Father always seemed to drill later in the spring than neighbouring farmers, for he believed another old country saying, so he said, that no barley should be sown 'until you can sit down in a field and the soil feels warm to your naked bottom.' Yet despite that conviction, I never saw him test the temperature of the land in that way himself.

When we children grew tired of watching the work, there were plenty of other pastimes to pursue with our friends. Clambering over roof tops, watching mosquito larvae in water butts, playing football and cricket, or ranging over the nearby fields and spinneys. The farm was an ideal place on which to live.

Life did not revolve entirely around the farm, however, for both Mother and Father came from large families, and as a result there were always numerous aunts and uncles to be visited, or various relatives would drop in on us. When in Cambridge, which in term-time was full of pallid, spotty youths wearing gowns and riding bicycles, we would often call in at the main butcher's shop. This was in Mill Road, a busy thoroughfare dissecting a large area of narrow streets and terraced houses that contrasted sharply with the elegant houses and large gardens elsewhere in the town, which belonged to college dons. The shop had sawdust on the floor, meat hanging in the windows, and behind was the small factory where there was always warmth and the smell of newly baked meat pies. Below, in the cellar, sausages were made, and we would watch intrigued as a happy balding great-uncle would allow a long sausage, cold and slippery, to slither snakelike from the nozzle of a sausage machine. Then, with a series

18

of skilful twists and flicks he would turn the one long sausage into a string of smaller ones.

Father's two half-brothers both worked in the butchery business; they occasionally wore the traditional striped and bloodstained aprons of the butcher, wielding knives and saws to cut joints for customers, but usually, with pens behind their ears and worry on their faces, they delved into wads of paper, peered into filing cabinets, and seemed inseparable from the office furniture. He also had three half-sisters, all several years his senior; they were big, buxom, laughing women, who mothered him, and smothered us with their benevolence.

Alfred was his younger brother, to whom during childhood he had been very close. Uncle Alfred was pale, bald, 'with a head like a bladder of lard', and jovial, he had an efficient wife, a liking for business, and bad eyesight. His trouble was that his eyes continually wavered to and fro, very slightly, and although the condition was hardly noticeable, it prevented him from focusing properly on anything. Life for him without glasses would have been like living in a world of swirling sea mist, and even with glasses he could not see well enough to drive a car and had to take up riding a bicycle. During the war, much to everyone's surprise he actually managed to pass a medical examination and join the army, but fortunately he was then called up before a doctor who knew him and shortly afterwards was discharged. Apparently it was considered that with a gun in his hand, even with his glasses on, he would have been a greater danger to his own side than to the Germans.

Mother's brothers were completely different and all worked on the land, two of them for my grandmother, Mrs Crow, on a farm some six miles away at Gills Hill, and the other one was self-employed. Jack was the eldest and to my young eyes was a rough, tough, surly man, but to those of his own age he was popular, likeable and naturally gregarious. Although on leaving school he had worked for my grandmother, he later started an agricultural contractor's business, with a large caterpillar tractor and heavy drainage equipment. He made a lot of money, but as he lived life to the full, he spent all he earned, and sometimes more. He rode a horse, and one winter's day he terrified me by galloping up and down the road cracking his long leather whip. He also rode motorbikes, which became his main obsession in life, and as his bank balance grew steadily smaller, his bikes became progressively bigger, better, and faster; he raced them all over the country, collecting silver trophies by the dozen.

Eventually he decided to give up racing and planned to ride for the last time in the September Grand Prix, on the Isle of Man in 1951. But even then he almost failed to arrive, as he had run out of money. Late on the evening before he was due to leave, he called on Father to explain his position, and was paid a cheque for some ploughing that he had done. The money was promptly banked and he left as planned. When lying eighth in the race he crashed into a brick wall at ninety miles an hour and was so badly smashed up that the doctors dared not remove his helmet. The following day he died.

The other two brothers, Cyril and Roy, I liked, and visits to or from them were always welcomed. Cyril was a tanned sportsman, a keen cricketer and good with a gun, who, because of his Cambridgeshire drawl, was often mistaken for an Australian. He was married and lived in a small farm cottage a hundred yards away from the large red brick, grey-tiled farmhouse where Uncle Roy lived with Grandmother. Uncle Roy worked and courted hard, but was worried by the fact that his hair had started to fall out. Between them the two brothers farmed extremely well.

We enjoyed visiting the farm, as it had ponds, turkeys and a tall Dutch barn, but we did not like the farmhouse. It was an ugly building, austere on the outside, dark and gloomy on the inside, with attics full of Victorian bric-a-brac, and landings where there were glass cases full of gaudy stuffed birds. Great-grandfather, bearded and severe, also lived there for his last few years, and was not amused one day when I asked Mother why he had straw growing on his face. He spent hours with a couple of old cronies sitting on a wooden bench at the roadside, close to a small spinney, and, convinced by the mischievous tales told by my cousins, I firmly believed until I was eight or nine years old that all woods were inhabited by sinister old men. Consequently I would never go into even the smallest wood alone, and once Cousin John and his sisters amused themselves greatly by deserting me in the middle of the spinney where the cronies were said to live.

Like the items in the attics, great-grandfather was a typical product of Victorian England; a puritan, a sabbatarian and a teetotaller. His beard had resulted from the fact that he refused to shave on Sundays, he considered shaving to be work, and as he visited the corn market every Saturday, arriving home too late in the evening to use his razor, he stopped shaving altogether. Occasionally, when his eyes or gums played him up, one of his old friends would take a selection of false teeth and glasses, acquired from departed relatives and acquaintances, to the spinney seat, and invariably a set of teeth or a pair of glasses was found to overcome his difficulties. Another strange habit he had was that of disappearing into a small outbuilding for what seemed like hours on end. That too was of red brick, with ivy climbing up the sides and a wall in front which prevented us from seeing what occupied him inside, and in summer it was surrounded by flies. One day after we observed him leave that strange building and make off towards the spinney we cautiously looked inside, and there to our astonishment, was a large wooden lavatory. Two seats were joined together over a deep pit, that bacteria never allowed to fill, and a pile of newspapers were in the corner instead of a toilet roll. We could not imagine why our aged relative should use this place when a flush toilet had been installed in the farmhouse, neither could we understand why there was more than one seat, for surely two people would not go to the lavatory together, sitting side by side?

The inclusion of that disreputable place in the farmhouse garden seemed strange, especially in view of the prim and proper manners of my grandmother. She was an extremely able woman, who after her early widowhood had run a farm and brought up her children with care and affection. In addition to her farm and household duties she helped run the local chapel, she collected money for missionaries, supported an organisation that aided sailors in distress, went 'Christmas singing', and as if that were not enough, she spent hours doing tatting and crochet. Lace-like shawls and table cloths would grow as her spools and hooks worked speedily and skilfully, pulling and tying the thread, and creating intricate patterns of great complexity and beauty. Credit for the way in which she coped was attributed to the after dinner sleep that she insisted upon having every day, which was a deep-rooted family custom.

Until the age of twenty-five, when she married, grandmother had been protected from all evil thoughts and deeds by her parents. Indeed it was not until after her wedding that she discovered that babies did not arrive in the doctor's bag; she then had five children in quick succession. She was also a very determined woman and was a non-swimmer until well over forty, then, while accompanying us on a holiday to Cromer she decided to learn to swim and managed easily. Before entering the sea, she would kneel at the water's edge, her water-wings already in place, and splash herself until cold enough to take the full plunge.

Every Christmas the whole Crow family would join together at the farmhouse for its annual get-together. The reunion would start at dinner time when all the brothers, sisters, in-laws and offspring, would sit at a large table and devour a goose, a cockerel, mounds of vegetables, a variety of sauces and a Christmas pudding smothered in burning brandy.

After the meal, the children would run off its effects outside, while the adults fell asleep around a large log fire; an enormous tea, with crackers, would follow, after which there would be games in the drawing-room. The climax of the evening was always charades, in which we were all expected to take part, and which were considered as much part of Christmas as the Christmas dinner.

The last such festive gathering took place when I was four or five years old. Cousin John, older and bigger than me, knew that I was easily frightened, and not satisfied at deserting me in the spinney during the afternoon, proceeded to antagonise me for the rest of the day. Late in the evening as the adults were preparing to leave for their respective homes and were collecting our coats, we children were left waiting by the fire. Because of the lull John decided to have some more entertainment; he put the poker into the fire, until it glowed bright red, and then holding it near my face he threatened to burn me. I screamed, much to his delight, and this routine was repeated several times. Finally he tired of his sport, and while his attention was elsewhere, I picked up the still glowing poker and ran it down his right arm. Bedlam followed; it was his turn to shriek, at real not imaginary pain, and as anxious adults tried to soothe his simmering burns, I pleaded, without much success, a case of self-defence.

Shortly after that Uncle Cyril and his family moved into the farmhouse, grandmother moved into his cottage, and that was the last time the season of peace and goodwill was spent at Gills Hill.

CHAPTER 2

The Village

———

Beyond the farm and the family was the village, with its origins going back hundreds of years into antiquity through Norman invasion, Saxon settlement, and Roman occupation. Parts of the past could still be seen, in the ancient tower of the church, the meadowland with its ridges and furrows caused by the strip farming husbandry of earlier generations, and the small gravel pits and sheep dips, fallen into disuse, that could be found throughout the parish.

The farms and fields provided work for most of the men, and sometimes the women too would gather potatoes or pick fruit to earn extra money. Nearly all the farms were like our own, with live-stock for eggs, meat and milk, and labourers to work the land. Hedges of elm, hawthorn, and creeping banks of bramble, surround-ed the small meadows, which in summer filled with buttercups, lush pasture and the grating sounds of amorous grasshoppers. In the north of the parish, chalk pushed its way up through the clay to form a small hill, and a spring bubbled from it, clear and cool, even during times of drought. There, the fields grew larger and above the corn and ploughland larks would disappear heavenwards, singing. This open span of eternity stretched over the whole village in a vast expanse of lowland sky, that constantly changed with night and day, with season, and with weather. In it, the sun and wind were as artist and artisan, with the wind moulding and casting the clouds, and the sun tinting and touching, shading and shining, against a backcloth of ever-varying blue. High cirrus clouds would be twisted and pulled into feathery fantasies, and mackerel skies would be flecked with deli-cate shades of pink and mauve. Effulgent towers of spuming white would grow and trek from one horizon to another and occasionally huge black anvils would shadow the land with thunder and fear.

24

Dusks and dawns were times when the heavens would fill with promises and warnings, in great tracts of colour and beauty; primrose shafts of light would cut through and disperse the fragments of early morning cloud, or the sun might set as a ball of angry naked flame.

The village itself was to the south of the parish, a mixture of trees and rooftops, scattered and amorphous; small thatched cottages with low doorways and wooded gardens, two rows of council houses, formal on the outside, but warm and comfortable inside, two pubs, a school, one church, a chapel, the village institute, and a few large houses, the homes of professional people and those with private means. Open ditches, sometimes choking with watercress, bordered the High Street and grass verges divided the path from the road. On one side, in a patch of scrub, stood an old shed covered with creosote, where every Tuesday, Friday and Saturday, Sidney Moden the blacksmith shoed horses and mended implements. At one time the local smith had lived and worked wholly in the village, and Moden's predecessor was said to have been a man of great skill, who, at the time of the Boer War had looked after the horses of Winston Churchill in South Africa. Since those days, work had declined, and Moden had to visit several villages in order to earn his living. However, on those days when the smithy was open, part of the High Street would be full of the smell of singed hoof and the metallic ringing of heavy hammers on the battered anvil. As he worked, with sleeves rolled up, sweat on his face, and a soiled apron flapping loosely down his front, I would sometimes watch, absorbed, on my way home from school. Sparks would fly in diffuse and dying  galaxies as he took white hot shoes from the forge and hammered them into shape, and then, as he plunged them into a tank of cold water, they would hiss and splutter, and disappear behind a cloud of steam. Once he would work all day long, trimming hooves, fitting shoes, hammering and twisting nails as the large old cart horses on which he worked stood patiently by, but gradually as the noise of tractors and trailers with pneumatic tyres replaced the sound of hooves and tumbrill carts, so he seemed to work less and less, and then he stopped coming altogether.

The High Street was the focal point of the village, with the White Horse at one end and the village pond and the Hoops at the other. The old bakery and the chapel stood to provide the physical and spiritual needs of the street, although the parish church, ascetic and established, also laid its claim to the souls and devotions of men. It stood, surrounded by gravestones, overlooking the chapel and to help win over the waverers, it administered the village school and charity. Sooner or later everybody had to pass through the High Street; to school, to shop, to pray, or to labour. Before we could reach it we had to cross the main road to Cambridge, which ran past the farm, and walk over the Leys (pronounced 'lays').

Not only was the name strange, but the Leys itself was also unusual, being a strip of rough grassland about a quarter of a mile long and fifty yards wide. Because of its shape, and the romantic fancies of local historians and college dons it was said to be an old archery butt, where in former times the loyal men of the village had practised their skills in case of war. But the older villagers smiled knowingly at this learned suggestion, and knew it simply to be an odd strip of land left over at the time of the enclosures, which, over the years had become common ground. Cottages, tall elms, and sprawling brambles, marked one boundary, an unkempt hedge of thorn another, with the High Street at the northern end and the main road to the south. The grass was coarse and tough through years of neglect, and in June and July, clumps of fingers and thumbs, (Birdsfoot trefoil) would appear as patches of vivid saffron. It would have made a useful meadow, and Father frequently hired it as additional summer grazing for his cows. This was unpopular with some of the village mothers, for children liked to play where they imagined archers had once shot their arrows, and as they ran and rolled about they were covered, not with a glory from the past, but with something much worse that the cows had left behind.

Strangers would sometimes be seen resting at one end of the Leys, for both tramps and gypsies were common. Men of the road would occasionally come to our door and ask for food, with their lined, dirty faces, making them seem like visitors from another world. Mother would never give them money, believing as she did that it was always spent on beer, but they never left hungry, usually getting a thick slice of bread and margarine, a chunk of cheese, a mug of tea, and sometimes a piece of cake. We would watch from a discreet distance while they ate, and they would show their gratitude by clearing up even the smallest crumbs and smiling with satisfaction. Some of the men would stay in the neighbourhood for several days, sleeping in barns, or erecting temporary shelters from broken branches and grass, but most passed straight through. All wore the shabbiest of clothes, buttonless and full of holes, and their hats and shoes were

generally in tatters. Once, while waiting on the railway bridge for a train that never came, I was terrified by one such wanderer who suddenly appeared from the middle of a clump of bushes. He had a dark luxuriant beard, dishevelled curly hair, and a long black coat, tied round the waist with string; he looked completely wild. My heart pounded with fear as he emerged, but he ignored me, slung his small bundle on his back and made off along the road. Most of the village children distrusted tramps, but it was the gypsies who were really feared, for they passed through in quite large numbers every year, on their way to Midsummer Common in Cambridge for the annual fair, or to the Fens for land work. Although the women, with their bright scarves, coloured dresses, and ornaments made from golden sovereigns, bore us no malice, we looked upon them as malign monsters who stole children and the sight of caravans overflowing with curly haired, ruddy faced infants seemed to confirm our fears. Even their horses and brightly painted caravans resting peacefully at camp could not persuade us otherwise, and adults often multiplied our misgivings by talking of didecoys, (a word used for travelling dealers and scrap merchants, implying that they were not true gypsies and could not be trusted) deception and theft.

Usually, however, the village was a place where the sights and sounds of everyday life led to feelings of security and wellbeing; women hanging out their washing, old men leaning on garden gates, Bert the postman delivering the letters, the roadman and the policeman on their rounds, and a variety of friendly faces passing on the gossip. Some three hundred and fifty people lived in the parish, a mixture of educated and ignorant, satisfied and sour, pious and pagan. A few of the younger men were more ambitious than their elders and sought to free themselves from their rustic roots by obtaining work in Cambridge as college servants or local government clerks. Every morning they would travel by bicycle or bus into town and as their status and prospects improved, so signs of their growing affluence appeared. A civil servant bought himself one of the first motor scooters, sleek and blue, and John and myself looked on it with envy as he demonstrated it to us. Not to be outdone, others began to commute in even grander style, in Morris Eights and Fords, and a new pattern of work and travel began to develop.

Most of the older men scorned 'pen pushing' and the nine to five jobs to be found in the 'holiday camps', and were content both with their lot and with their lives on the land. They had no wish for anything different. As I heard them talk to Father, or among themselves, their memories seemed to transcend the world in which I lived and go back into history. They would recall times when they saw the first aeroplanes, airships and motorcars and as they talked, the old pictures in my scrap book would surge to life and roar across the skies where Meteor jets and giant American B36s now flew, or an ancient car would chug along the High Street, with a man carrying a red flag walking at the front. They spoke, too, of times when they were hungry, of relatives going into the workhouse, when children collected acorns to sell to farmers as pig food, and when their fathers had scythed corn at 3s 6d an acre or been hired for 4d a day. Jim could even remember back to the times when he was ten or eleven years old, and a pair of oxen were regularly driven along the road past his home and used as a team for ploughing; when their master stopped for 'docky', they would lie down and ruminate contentedly until he was ready to continue. ('Docky' was a break for refreshment at 10am – usually tea and a sandwich, kept in a docky bag – the name derived from the fact that when farm workers first stopped for this break, their wages were 'docked' for the time spent eating and not working, hence 'docky').

Many of the men had spent the whole of their working lives on various farms, from the age of twelve or thirteen, and had lived through an era when silence and the noises of the countryside were the only accompaniment to toil, when men worked the fields to the sound of horses breathing and the plodding of hooves, when the ploughshares could be heard cutting into the soil, which would crunch and crumble as it turned over into its furrow. The old steam ploughs that between the wars had ploughed six or eight furrows at a time were also remembered with affection, but even they had been quiet compared with the noise of combustion that now invaded the fields and which each year grew louder. They looked back with feelings of nostalgia and achievement, but not with regret.

Mr Disbrey was typical of this breed of countryman; Mother insisted that we called virtually everybody mister or missus, as a sign of respect. He had been brought up as a child in one of the thatched cottages overlooking the Leys, and now lived in a brick and tiled bungalow in the High Street. He was a small man from a large family, quiet, hard-working and a regular church-goer. When he was not working he always seemed to be walking, and each week he covered miles on foot, just watching and absorbing the things around him. Although alert and intelligent, his parents had been too poor to send him or his brother George to grammar schools, which their intellects merited, but nevertheless he became more literate than many of the 'educated' and wrote poems and short stories for his own amusement and that of his children. He had left school in his early teens, and began his working life by walking five or six miles every morning to work on a hay trusser, a contraption that tied hay into bundles, after which he spent his time working on local farms. One dark night during his childhood he could remember looking out of his bedroom window and seeing the vicarage on fire beyond the Leys and the High Street. Horse-drawn fire engines galloped out from Cambridge to fight the blaze with water pumped from the village pond, but the building was gutted. The church bells also rang on in his memory, for whenever they were heard tolling, slowly and dolefully, it was a sign that death had come. If the toll was regular, it meant that a child had died, but if it came in twos it was for a woman, and in threes, a man. Before the melancholy sound finally stopped, there would be a pause, and then the age of the departed would be rung out.

But he also remembered happier occasions, of the village 'tug of war' team, that trained by tying one end of its rope around the trunk of a large tree, and heaving and straining until it was fit enough to dispose of all the challengers from the surrounding area. There were social occasions too, dances and whist drives at the village institute, and quoits at the Hoops, where men threw large metal rings some twenty yards through the air into a pit of gault, the one landing closest to a small metal peg being the winner. Another highlight of the village year was Plough Monday, the first Monday after January 6th (old Christmas Day), by which time all the ploughing was supposed to have been completed, and the farm workers could celebrate. In the evening groups of men would go round the village cracking their horse whips, shouting, laughing and singing: 'Plough Monday

Plough, plough up your houses, plough down your doors, play for an 'a'penny, for a poor old plough boy.' They would knock on doors and collect money to buy beer, for it was a time of uninhibited and unsophisticated enjoyment. Occasionally, two old friends from another village would stagger over to the Hoops, they needed no special occasion or encouragement to celebrate, and were nearly always drunk. They would become so inebriated that on leaving the bar they would collapse on a grass verge or settle into the bottom of a hedge, where they would spend long cold nights in alcoholic oblivion. Sometimes they remained where they had fallen until well into the following morning and it was not unknown for them to be found by early morning workmen, still sleeping and covered with frost. Horkey was another time for eating and drinking, when, to celebrate the completion of harvest, some of the farmers would throw parties for their men at which beer flowed freely and food was plentiful. It was at this time of year that gleaners became a familiar sight in the fields and as soon as the sheaves and shocks had been carted, the poorer members of the village would go searching for ears of corn that had been left behind in the stubble. Wearing special aprons into which they would put all they found, they would usually collect enough grain to keep their few hens fed throughout the winter, or if they wanted money, they would sell their gleanings to one of the local millers.

Sport, too, was important in village life; cricket was especially popular and one solitary football match took place every year on Boxing Day morning. The men would gather on the Leys in their working boots, pick two teams, put coats down for goal posts, and then play amongst themselves. On that day Mr Disbrey's father would disappear into the White Horse from 10am until 10pm, where he would drink beer and eat free mince pies in front of an open log fire. The pub was run by two sisters, the 'Miss Webbs', who had taken it over from their father, a publican who had not only sold beer, but also brewed it. Although Mr Disbrey remembered these people and events with pleasure, and could keep listeners enthralled for as long as he cared to talk, he had no wish to go back to the conditions of his younger days, for he could see changes that he welcomed, ones which gave men money when they were sick, shorter working hours, comfort and security in their old age.

From the very beginning, Mother discouraged us from going near either pub, for she had signed the 'pledge', a promise of abstinence, while a child, and imagined them to be places of the most appalling wickedness and debauchery. If we ever queried this, our attention was drawn to an old man with a moustache, cap, striped shirt and a waistcoat, who always seemed to be leaning on his gate, waiting for opening time. He was fat, slow, and indolent, and we were led to believe that all who ventured into pubs grew up to be just like him.

By the time I started school, only one of the 'Miss Webbs' remained, and she had retired to live in a small cottage in the High Street. Her house was cov-
ered with straggling climbing plants and hidden in a large garden, overgrown with bushes, shrubs and trees. She seemed to be extremely ancient, with a pale, wrinkled and whiskery face, from which stared a pair of watery sullen eyes, and she always wore black; a black hat, a long black dress, thick black stockings and black plimsolls. On my way to school I would always hurry past her garden, for sometimes she could be seen crouching behind bushes or trees, spying on people as they

went by. Because of her appearance and behaviour we suspected that she was a witch.

Sometimes we children would gather at the end of the Leys by the High Street, for on the other side of the road was a field owned by Miss Webb, which stretched to the back of her garden. It was a forbidden place, with a wooden fence and strands of rusting barbed wire preventing entry, but it was also an inviting place, with long grass and a number of quite large pollarded elms (also known locally as doddled elms), neglected and full of holes, in which jackdaws and owls liked to nest.

Every summer when the parent jackdaws flew in dizzy aerobatics, or rode in the swirling eddies of warm wind above the trees, our thoughts turned to their young, which we wanted as pets, and which we could only get by entering Miss Webb's forbidden field. From the security of the ditch between the Leys and the road we would survey the old lady's garden for movement, then, when convinced that it was safe to proceed, we would cross the road, climb carefully through the fence, and creep or crawl through the grass towards the elms. Invariably, just as the trees were reached there would be a shout, and Miss Webb would appear, running as fast as her plimsolls could carry her from the undergrowth in her garden, her hat still firmly in place, her dress billowing out behind her, and brandishing a large stick. We would flee in terror, ignoring scratches as we scrambled through or over the barbed wire, mount our bikes, and pedal furiously away.

It was with great consternation that one day I watched Ol' Ma Webb turn into our gateway and knock on the back door. Mother opened it, and Miss Webb asked if she could have some eggs delivered each week. She liked eggs, and during the war when they had been scarce, she had kept guinea fowl, which laid large clutches every spring and which if kept in a cool place, would keep for well over a year. Eggs were now more plentiful, however, the guinea fowl were no more, and much to my dismay Mother agreed to the old lady's request, and said that I would deliver them. My first journey along her overgrown path was full of fear. The shadows cast by the trees and dense shrubs were such that I expected the old crone in her black clothes to appear suddenly from nowhere, emerging from the darkness like a moribund practitioner of the occult, wanting to frighten a small boy with her mysterious powers. Much to my surprise, as the safety of the High Street receded, so the house appeared through the undergrowth in a small clearing bathed in sunlight, with tall holly-hocks growing by the door. Inside Miss Webb was not stirring some noxious witch's brew as I had expected, but was sitting contentedly in a large armchair in front of a coal fire. The furniture was old, with pots and pans on ledges and window sills, and when she saw that I had brought the eggs she actually smiled, a broad and toothless smile.

This egg delivery continued unhindered until one day when, cycling across the Leys, late for school, my knee caught Miss Webb's basket and two dozen eggs crashed to the path. They were nearly all smashed, and the few that were not, were so badly cracked that they could never be sold. Unfortunately there was no time to return for more, and in any case Mother would have been angry at my careless-ness, so I carefully scraped up all the bits and pieces, oozing and slimy with egg white and broken yolk, and put them back into the basket placing the nearly whole ones at the top. I knocked on the door, handed the old lady the basket as usual, and hurried away before she had time to study the contents. That evening she again came to see Mother and gave back the still dripping basket. I had to explain my misfortune, and she was given two dozen more.

It was not long after this that she set the whole village talking by going on her first holiday abroad, still in her hat and plimsolls, to the Passion Play at Oberammergau. This journey was particularly strange since she rarely went to church, and it became even stranger when shortly after her return, she died suddenly. Then the gossip really started, for this lady who had spent most of her life selling alcohol, and who had never been very devout, left nearly all her land and money to the parish church to provide a larger income for the parson. Those who believed in miracles claimed that she had under-gone a dramatic and sudden conversion as she saw death approaching, while the cynics believed that as she had spent her working life in league with the Devil, she was now trying to buy her way into heaven.

Although some fields had been owned by Miss Webb, and others were the property of Father and a few small farmers, most of the land in the neighbourhood was owned by the colleges, and a wealthy country gentleman named Herbert Holben. He lived in the village, was much respected, and became the self-appointed village squire. He was very old, frequently unshaven, and I would often see him out for walks with 'his man Jackson', on whom he would lean when tired. He wore a cap, a long brown coat, and blew his nose by placing his thumb and index finger, one on each nostril, and blowing hard; a habit Mother told us we must never follow, but which, when we were sure nobody was looking, we would sometimes try.

The house in which old Holben lived was built in 1880, by his uncle 'Lawyer' Holben, a tall, moral man, 'as upright as a yard of pump water', for the then enormous sum of £3,000. It was constructed with red bricks similar to those used in the farmhouse at Gills Hill, but was much larger, and designed to show all passers-by that it was the residence of a gentleman. Despite its ostentatious grandeur it failed to incorporate the charm of the more traditional houses and cottages, and it was obvious that it had been built as a monument to impress, rather than as a home in which to live.

Looking out over the front lawn were enormous bay windows, and even the ordinary windows were adorned with decorative stone work. Four chimney stacks, two of them castellated, grew from the roof where there were gables with cornices of ornamental masonry and smooth grey slates which rose and fell like a miniature range of folded mountains. Large oak doors in an archway of stone, resembling the cavernous jaws of some great animal, opened inwards into the hall, where on dark December nights in the past, small boys had sung carols on the steps outside while the squire stood bathed in light in the open door-way. Inside, a staircase swept down from a balcony above, and

rooms with large open fireplaces, corridors, a kitchen and maids, all fought with the cold and the draughts to keep the master and the mistress happy.

Behind the house was a courtyard, with outbuildings; a dove-cote, a garage and stables, and surrounding all was a large garden, with rose beds, vegetables, lawns, and a great variety of fully mature trees. The whole thing was like an extravagant Victorian folly, with the towering conifers, dark and forbidding, always making it seem inhospitable.

Jackson had to attend to both the master and the garden, and wherever the old man's shuffle took him, Jackson had to follow. All his life Mr Holben had been a keen sportsman; when in the army he had ridden horses and become an expert in lancing pegs while at full gallop. For this feat he was called Pegger, a nickname that stayed with him all his life. On returning to civilian life he took up shooting and attended shoots both near and far and, in addition, he would scour his own ground for any signs of game. As his shuffle became progressively more laboured and his reflexes slowed, he still refused to yield to the inevitable and continued to shoot. Jackson would accompany him to Warner's Corner, a large fifty-acre field which he had once owned and which now belonged to Father, and there he would try and continue his sporting life. The field was surrounded by ideal

game cover, at one end there were hedges, willows, and the brook, along one side was a cart track and scrubland, and along the other was a small spinney. In the field itself there were patches of pasture and kale, which was cut by hand as winter fodder for the cows. It attracted numerous pheasants, partridges, rabbits and hares, and when something came within range, Jackson would help the old man to aim, support him to prevent the recoil knocking him over, and Holben would pull the trigger.

Although I only saw him in later years, stories of his earlier days, both fact and fiction, abounded, and were a frequent feature of conversation whenever people had time to spare and wanted a good laugh. Before he was overtaken by the dulling and humiliating process of time, Pegger was said to have been extremely active in the village, speaking with the accent of a gentleman and raising his hat to all the ladies he met. Virtually everywhere he went his dogs went too and even when reading the lesson at church, his favourite golden labrador would follow him to the lectern and lie at his feet until it was time to return to the pew. Grandmother regarded him with the utmost respect, for shortly after being widowed, while she was still living in the village, Mr Holben had called on her, in his long brown coat, raised his hat, and offered to give her a pony for her children. An offer that she readily accepted, and which brought a smile back to her face for the first time since her bereavement.

There is no doubt that he was a charming, well-liked man, bearing his wealth and good breeding with modesty, but at the same time setting an example in honest business, morality and dignity. He was, however, the cause of much gossip, for although he had his good points, he was obsessively mean with his money and, much to the amusement of the villagers, he also collected birds' eggs. It is true that his house presented an external facade of high living, but inside both he and his wife lived most frugally, believing that if they looked after all their halfpennies and pennies, the pounds really would look after themselves; consequently the only time he spent money freely and without regret was when he went bird-nesting.

His quest for new eggs took him all over the world; to America, where he grew a beard because he considered the cost of shaving to be excessive; to Morocco, where he paid his guides so poorly that on one occasion when he was suspended by a rope over a precipice, examining a nest, they refused to pull him up again until he promised to increase their wages. In Bulgaria and Spain he saw the inside of local jails for trespass. But his greatest trip and the pinnacle of his oological career was said to have been a visit to Iceland, where, while walking along a track, he fell headlong into a ditch and landed next to a frozen egg of the extinct great auk, the last such egg ever to have been found. It was also rumoured that before he started out on his world-wide search for eggs, he had all his teeth extracted, because he had heard that foreign dentists charged exorbitant rates.

When Father was in his teens, many of the local children had earned extra pocket money by collecting eggs for Pegger, not just one egg taken from each nest, but whole clutches and sometimes the actual nest as well. As a result, his beloved egg collection was enormous, with glass case after glass case containing nothing but eggs; whole clutches stolen from magpies, jays, rooks, jackdaws and a wide variety of both rare and common birds. While his overawed visitors were shown all the variations in colour and size of his latest prizes, somewhere deprived birds would be fretting in a summer of frustration and impotence.

The idea of the village squire, with his money, his books and his learning, going bird-nesting was considered to be most eccentric, but the tales that really entertained the village, which were eagerly sought and quickly passed on, were the ones concerning his chronic miserliness; for his saving, thrift and self-denial were not just passing fancies, but a way of life. Even his loyal man Jackson would comment, incredulously, after some new economy had been devised: 'He's a gentleman in his manners but mean in his money.' For Pegger considered that nothing was too inconvenient or degrading if it saved him a few pence; he wore his clothes until they could be repaired no more, he grew as much of his own food in his garden as was possible, saving any seeds, including pips from rotten tomatoes, and before embarking upon any course of action he always counted the cost. He ate all he shot – all, that is, except herons – for after shooting one that had an eel lodged down its throat, he left those birds alone as he disliked eels. Even his gun-dogs cost him little money, for he fed them mainly on scraps and waste that he scrounged from other people. Charlie Murkin once kept goats, and on being presented with a new male kid which he could not keep, he killed it and buried it in the garden. Soon afterwards there was a knock on the front door of his council house, and there was Mr Holben, again with his long brown coat and hat: 'Ah Mr Murkin, I understand that your goat has just given birth to a kid you don't want,' and he persuaded Charlie to dig it up and give it to him, so that he could feed it to his dogs. Again, when he heard that a local cat had given birth to kittens, he got them too, boiled them up in a large pot, and his dogs had an even tastier meal.

It was in the little things that he really concentrated his saving. When he was given a box of overripe damsons, he removed all the rotten specks with a knife, so that they should not be wasted, and on his return from America, when he arrived at the station, rather than telephoning for a taxi, he donned his overcoat and struggled with his cases and trunk over a mile to his home. During the winter, however, he occasionally journeyed in the opposite direction, from house to the station, for his coal was delivered by horse and cart from the station yard. After each delivery he would carefully retrace the cart's route in case any lumps of coal had fallen off. If, during his walk, he found any old shoes or boots in addition to coal, he would collect them as well, to remove the hobnails for future use and to store the leather in case it should ever be needed.

Moden was once asked to call at the big house, to inspect a leaking tap which was quickly diagnosed as washer trouble. Rather than go to the expense of a new washer, Mr Holben suggested that a leather one should be cut from his store of old boots; being a blacksmith and not a plumber, a leather worker, or junk collecter, Moden insisted that as he was to do the job he was to do it properly. But even after a metal washer had been fitted his problems were not over, for when it was time for payment, Mr Holben offered to pay him, not with money, but with sticks of rhubarb cut from his garden.

The blacksmith was offered rhubarb on another occasion too, for Pegger decided that it would be a saving if he managed his own shoe repairs, and for this he needed a hobbing iron. Most families possessed one of these so that they could do simple repairs, consequently hobbing irons could be purchased quite cheaply. Mr Holben had no wish to buy one, however, instead he found an old plough coulter lying rusting in a field, and took it in to Moden, asking him to bend it into the required shape. Using his forge, his hammer and his sweat, Moden bent the metal as desired. 'Oh, thank you Moden, how can I pay you?' the squire asked on collecting it. 'Would you like some rhubarb?'

'I'll think about it,' Moden muttered and continued his work. Unfortunately he was working with his back to the door, bending over the hind leg of a horse, which he held between his knees while working on the hoof. After a pause, thinking that Holben had gone, he mimicked sarcastically: 'Would you like some rhubarb Moden? I'd like to get his bloody rhubarb and stick it up his bloody great ...'

Alas. Mr Holben was still there: 'Really Moden, really, you shouldn't use words like that!'

In his shooting he saw other means of saving money. At Michaelmas, it was customary for landlords to give their tenants the present of a shilling. Mr Holben was different, he gave them all a rabbit, but even then not a whole rabbit, for invariably he would remove the 'innards' first, to feed to his dogs. On arriving by bicycle at a local shoot, since his car remained almost permanently in its garage, he found that he had a puncture and asked the gamekeeper to mend it. At the end of the day, instead of receiving a tip, the flabbergasted man was given a shot plover to compensate him for his time and trouble.

Even when out for walks, any bits of wood he found were carried home to burn, and after a barn caught fire and was gutted, he searched among the ashes and the charred remains for any old nails that could be recovered. But all these exercises in thrift paled into insignificance when compared with the saving he made in his toiletry requirements, for he rarely bought a toilet roll. Instead, he tore conveniently sized paper squares from his daily newspaper, *The Daily Telegraph*, then, if they were not too soiled after use, he would dry them in front of the fire and use them again.

During the time when he actively farmed, Mr Holben was just as careful in his work as he was in his leisure. After harvest, when the stacks were built and thatched, he would send his two maids with scissors and a sack to cut off all the ears of corn that protruded outwards and might spoil. In fact, from all the many stories of his money mania, there was only one which showed him being outmanoeuvred in business, and that was by grandfather.

Early one summer, grandfather bought some hay from Pegger, collecting it off the field in tumbrill carts loaded by Bob Mallows, a man who had worked on the farm for many years and who preceded Jim. Although Mallows was a good loader, Mr Holben thought that the field should be cleared faster, and when Bob said: 'I think we've got enough on the load now, sir,' Holben replied: 'There's plenty of room yet, Mallows, plenty of room yet.'

'Plenty of room where, sir?'

'Why there's plenty of room upwards Mallows, plenty of room upwards.'

Later in the year Holben wanted to sell a small stack of straw, but as grandfather considered that he had been over-charged for the hay, they could not agree a price. After much haggling it was decided that one cartload only should be bought and Mallows and another man were sent to fetch it. Remembering Mr Holben's words, an enormous load was gathered, so large that it required two cart ropes to hold it in place, and an additional horse to pull it home. When he wanted payment Holben walked round to where his stack had been and was astonished to find it had gone. Thinking that grandfather had decided to have more than one load he went to the farmyard and found both grandfather and Mallows: 'Ah, Mr Page, I see you decided to have the whole stack after all.'

'No, we only collected one load as agreed.'

'What, Mallows, surely you collected two.'

'No, sir,' replied Mallows, 'you remember what you said about there being plenty of room on a cart, sir?'

'Plenty of room on a cart where, Mallows?'

'Why, plenty of room upwards sir, plenty of room upwards.'

When the old man's shuffle finally stopped, and I noticed him no more about the village, it was possible to detect a genuine feeling of loss, for although he had been wealthy, well educated and eccentric, he was also regarded with real affection throughout the parish and mixed freely with everybody. Jackson had to look for fresh work and lamented: 'You couldn't help liking the old boy.' So Mr Holben passed on, his money and his eggs stayed behind, and the stories about him remained very much alive.

Halfway between Mr Holben's house and the farm, along the main road, was a small cluster of cottages and it was in one of these that Crabby lived; a man quite unlike the village squire. Whereas Pegger had been rich, learned, and hard-working, with a house akin to a mansion and his man Jackson to lean on, Crabby was poor, uneducated and idle, living in a small semi-detached tumbledown cottage, with only a stick or his garden gate to lean on. In fact, the only similarity between the two old men was in the way they cleared their nostrils, for Crabby, too, used his index finger and thumb, although with less skill for he frequently had to introduce the sleeve of his coat as an auxiliary aid. Every day his elderly, bent figure would call at the farm for milk and Father, with milk buckets and teat cups in a tankful of scalding water would stop his unpleasant task of washing up, to hand Crabby a can containing two pints.

During his working life, which had been interrupted by spells of unemployment as soon as dole money had been introduced, Crabby had been a shepherd, and it was said that what he didn't know about sheep wasn't worth knowing. As the work and wanderings of a shepherd depended on the changeable fancies of the elements, he could forecast the weather more accurately than most of the professional experts with their barometers, thermometers and wind gauges. In fact, he had nothing but contempt for both the new way of farming, in which his beloved sheep had been almost completely replaced by cattle, pigs and arable land, and for the new scientific age in general, which he could see usurping common sense and replacing individual skills with all kinds of nonsense. When he had been at work, he had castrated young sheep by slitting the scrotum with a penknife and biting out the testicles with his teeth; this simple operation had now been refined and it took two men, a surgical knife and a large bottle of disinfectant to do the same job. In medicine, too, he considered that things had developed for the worse as Doctor Simpson, the new village G.P., with his black bag and stethoscope, visited the sick and gave out pills or strange new prescriptions for the coughs and conditions he found. Crabby's mother had administered another kind of medicine in the village many years before, using vastly different principles in her unofficial practice, based not on science or the Hippocratic Oath, but on superstition, folk-lore and primitive psychology. He still possessed her old book of potions and brews, which pre-scribed mixtures of herbs, mice, toads and a whole variety of other ingredients for ailments that were likely to strike people down (as a boy, Crabby had eaten a mouse as a cure for whooping cough). Although her craft had died with her, Crabby still had a strong belief in her traditional ways, as had old Dut, who lived in the High Street and claimed that he could charm warts. This was substantiated by Father who told of a long-departed relation of ours who had once had a large wart on the end of his nose. On seeing the unfortunate great-uncle Fred, Dut exclaimed: 'Why you don't want that ol' thing there do you, master?' and he assured him that it would go away. Within a few days it had disap-peared completely. An old ditcher was another, Father recalled, who was said to have powers over man and beast. He claimed that he could distinguish the sex of calves before they were born by listening to the prospective mother's stomach, which one he never specified, and although he was nearly always wrong, he was never discouraged. He also told Father that he had once cured a woman of milk fever by poulticing her breasts with cow dung.

Across the road from Crabby was the small brick house in a large garden where Bert Nightingale lived with his crippled mother. She was old and confined to a large wooden armchair; he was middle-aged, a rotund and genial gardener who made a living by digging gardens and selling vegetables. He loved to remember the past, the times when he went along the hedgerows with his father, netting sparrows and blackbirds to put in pies, and how his father had threshed field beans with a flail which still stood up in the corner of the garden shed. However, he was not only interested in what had been, but was very much in touch with the present, and as he cycled about the village he picked up all the local news. Whenever a cow calved and Bert got to know, he would ask Father for a can of 'bisnings'. 'Bisnings' is the local pronunciation, correctly called 'beestings', the 'curds and whey' of Little Miss Muffet. It is the milk of a freshly calved cow, which is thick and yellow; when heated, with sugar, it sets and is similar to a sweet egg custard, that both he and his mother ate with relish.

Harry the cobbler lived three doors away, in the first of a row of council houses. He was the village cynic, a prophet of doom, who, in addition to his small shoe repair shop in Cambridge, kept a few pigs with the help of Charlie Murkin. Whenever he spoke it was usually to announce some imminent disaster that was likely to befall his shop or knock the bottom out of the pig trade; but although in his business life he could see nothing but despair, in things unconnected with his bank balance he could see some good and became a keen painter in oils. Unfortunately, his artistic aspiration was greater than his powers of observation, and he presented Father with a picture of the farmyard that had a strange horned beast peering from one of the sheds and the sun setting in the north.

Between the cobbler and the gardener was the post office, which was run by another Bert and was the village centre for trade in goods and gossip. There, stories true and false concerning births, marriages and deaths were told, listened to and passed on, and those with much to tell could spend half an hour or more just buying a 2d stamp. Bert was also the postman, who cycled every day at a leisurely pace round the village. From the envelopes and cards he delivered he got to know who was writing to whom, who banked where, what was happening everywhere, and how people were enjoying their holidays. As a continuous procession of people had to go to the post office for their stamps, pensions and postal orders, Bert converted the interior of his shop into that of a general store, with every available space being taken up with shelves, all overflowing with tins, packets of groceries, bottles of 'fizz', sweets and everything that a family was likely to need in the course of a week. Seeing him serving behind the counter, or delivering the letters on a warm afternoon, smiling and nodding to everyone he passed, made the job of postman the most attractive in the village.

The other shop in the High Street was completely different. In the old days it had been the village bakery where Charlie had started work and where, at the age of thirteen, he had carried sacks containing nineteen stone of beans on his back. But with the yard where horses and carts had once called and where flour and corn had been stored now empty, the only part still used was the shop, where groceries and confectionery were sold instead of bread. On entering, an old bell would sway and ring over the door and then all would be hushed until Mrs Creek shuffled into the dark interior from her living room at the back. The large shelves were nearly always half empty and old advertisements could be seen through the gloom proclaiming the wonders of Cherry Blossom Boot Polish, Farmers Glory Cornflakes and Camp Coffee Essence. The counter, which extended along three sides, was broad and high, and behind it the old lady would take an eternity to search out what was required. She sold mostly sweets, which were weighed out on an old set of balancing scales, and she would move sweets to and fro for minutes on end until the pans balanced. Sometimes, to get the correct weight, she would even bite a sweet in two, putting one half on the scales and returning the other to the bottle. She was similarly meticulous when weighing out cheese, using the smallest crumbs and slivers as make-weights, and when getting a pound of tomatoes, the last one was always cut to the exact weight, to make sure that the customer got no more than was asked for. Consequently, most people shopped at the post office, making only occasional sympathy visits to Mrs Creek to buy small items. In fact, the only time that she was rushed off her feet was when sweet rationing was lifted for an experimental day; then people trooped into her shop and Mother gave us 6d each to spend on sweets and Mars bars.

Other traders came into the village during the week in a variety of vans and lorries; butchers and bakers competed eagerly for custom, as did grocers, the 'Corona man', occasional scissor grinders, and two old men on a yellow horse-drawn trailer who regularly drove through shouting: 'Rag an' bone. Rag an' bone.' Builders and carpenters, painters and ditchers, all found odd jobs at private houses or on the farms. Irishmen would call, offering to clean out ditches at piecework rates, and black mud and slime would fly through the air at such a speed that farmers always felt that they had priced the work too high. Possibly this was because the two local ditchers who were employed all the year round at the bottom of council ditches never gave the impression that speed was one of the main aspects of the job. Indeed, one of them who arrived on his bike each day from a neighbouring village, rode so slowly that he appeared to contradict all the normally

held concepts of time and motion, and seemed to defy the law of gravity itself. Riding by, with his coat buttoned up, cap pulled down over his eyes and his shovel and slasher over the handlebars, Chronicle's manner and bearing was entirely in keeping with that of guardian of the parish ditches. When he spoke, his voice was husky, as if affected by years of breathing in the damp air of numerous ditches and drains and whenever he passed me he always smiled and said: ''allo mate.'

But of all the workmen and traders that came to the village, those whose skill and way of life made them into almost an elite were the thatchers, and when we had to have the house re-thatched, the prospect was greeted with much excitement. When the work was in progress we would often stand looking upwards as the two men worked steadily and skilfully above: knocking up the thatch, pegging with hazel spits and covering it with wire to keep the sparrows away. Straw blew all over the lawns and garden, and the crocuses and daffodils seemed to match the colour of the new roof, which was orderly and clean, ready for another twenty-five years of unpredictable weather.

And so the village went on more or less as it had for many generations, with life and death, work and play, prayer and profanity, all playing their part. But as it possessed such a variety of buildings and people it had grown into something more than just a place in which to live, for it was, in a simple and practical sense, a community.

CHAPTER 3

God

———

There was, so we were taught from our earliest days, someone else who could be found in the parish, but who was not a member of either the village or the family; and that someone was God. We were given to understand that he was usually to be found up in Heaven, except on Sundays, when he would personally visit the chapel in the High Street. Some claimed, too, that he could be found in the parish church, but this we did not believe, and I gained the impression that behind its ancient walls strange, unwholesome practices took place, which although undertaken in God's name, in fact roused him to anger.

To some, God was a wise old sage, high up in the sky, who looked down upon his handiwork with sadness in his eyes, kindness in his heart and a long flowing beard that had remained uncut since time began. There were others to whom such a figure was most un-Godlike. They saw him as a divine sabbatarian despot, whose will they had to follow and whose laws they had to obey unquestionably. They imagined his celestial sycophantic minions, spying from their lofty pedestals on all those mortals far below, recording all our misdeeds and failings in gigantic ledgers, which would be opened and studied at a later date; at that time the bad deeds would be totalled up and offset against a similar record of good deeds, maintained by other angelic bodies, and on the result would be decided an eternity spent in Heaven or in Hell. But even so, their God was not content to sit back passively, and would sometimes actively participate in events on Earth. He would protect and safeguard members of his loyal flock, but would wreak havoc on all who transgressed, bringing poverty and disease to their families, and occasionally striking them with lightening.

A few had faith of a much more mystical nature; to them God was an omnipresent feeling of good, outside time and beyond mortal comprehension, who could be seen in the delicately fashioned petals of a rose, who breathed immortality into the newly born, who could be heard in the wind, and whose presence could be felt in the stillness of a starlit night. Only a very small number confessed to absolute disbelief; to them the man Jesus was nothing more than a character in a glorified fairy story, God was a fraud, 'and when you're dead, you're dead.'

Although God took on different forms for different people, or was even non-existent, yet his influence was universal and he affected the lives of believers and non-believers alike. On Sundays and special days the church bells would ring out, carrying the call to worship into every household, and nearly all holidays were holy days or connected in some way to the church. Then there were God's own personal representatives in the village, who would visit the aged and

the infirm, and who were often to be seen embarking upon some righteous deed. The vicar was a tall, bald-headed canon, who had preached only in village churches since the time of his ordination, and if he passed a chapel person, or a waverer, he would look down his nose and show clear signs of disapproval. His flock respected him as an educated man, whose long black cassock, dog collar, cross hanging from a chain around his waist, and the severe expression on his face, gave them the impression that he had a direct line of communication to God. The Baptist minister, on the other hand, was considered by some to be far inferior, for he did not possess the same dignity as the representative of the Established Church. To make matters worse, his voice bore no traces of a university education, but still carried the lilting inflexions of the Welsh valleys where he had spent his boyhood; he always wore an ordinary collar, and sometimes his short, fat body would even mount a rickety bicycle. An uneasy truce existed between the two men, both thinking of the other as a thoroughly bad influence.

Every Sunday they would climb into their respective pulpits, and that was the day when normal life in the village came to a halt. The post office and the shop remained closed, except at the back door, work on the farms stopped, even during harvest time; nobody would dare to kick a football about on the recreation ground, for play on a Sunday was considered to be as wicked as work, and it took a great deal of courage, or simple obduracy to defy this convention. Occasionally, somebody would wash their car or dig their garden on the Lord's Day, and prayers would be said in church and chapel asking God to punish those who sinned.

To us, God was a strange mixture. We were taught that it was his hand that created all things good, and which led us to sing hymns like 'All things bright and beautiful', and from this it naturally followed that whenever we were well-behaved, happy or helpful, he was pleased. At the same time we were reminded that whenever we erred, if we opened our eyes during grace, if we told tales or fought, he would become extremely angry. Consequently it was hard to have a clearly defined view of him in our minds, for he seemed to be a mixture of holy naturalist, benign old man, and awesome tyrant. To both Mother and Father his existence and presence were very real, and this reality they tried to pass on to us. We were told that he was a person who would listen when spoken to, but who would not always appear to reply, and we were assured that whenever we were in trouble he would come to our aid. To remind us of his goodness we had to say grace before every meal, and in the evening we were encouraged to say our prayers. When we were hungry, after a morning at play, grace was a chore; we would gabble it off as quickly as possible: 'Thank you for the food we eat, thank you for the flowers so sweet, thank you for the birds that sing, thank you God for everything, Amen,' and we hurriedly made a grab for our knives and forks.

Mother's faith in God had come to her through several generations of Baptists and Methodists, and was steeped in the traditions of Protestant dissent; a belief that preached purity and concern for the less fortunate. Alcohol, smoking, swearing, and an interest in certain forbidden regions of the human body, made up the four worst evils, and Sunday was the one day in the week entirely devoted to God. Consequently, Sundays were spent in almost exactly the same way as Mother had spent them in her childhood, and as her mother had done before her.

On that day we were not allowed to use our bicycles, the Hillman Minx that the firm had bought for use on the farm stayed in the garage, our toys had to stay in the cupboard, the television remained switched off, and we had no newspapers. The whole day seemed to be spent eating, and going to chapel. Breakfast was always at 9 o'clock, when we would each eat half a grapefruit, followed by fried sausages. We children would then rush around getting ready for Sunday School, putting on our smartest clothes and shoes that had been polished the night before. Sunday School and the walk home were followed by dinner; Yorkshire pudding and gravy, and then, served on the same plate, roast beef and vegetables. After a short rest, it was again time to trudge across the Leys and along the High Street for the 3 o'clock service. Tea nearly always consisted of egg and cress sandwiches, celery and sponge cake, and then, before we were considered old enough to attend the 6.30 service, Father would go to chapel by himself, and we would stay at home with Mother, who would supervise our own service in the drawing-room. Mother or big sister Mary would play the old piano accompaniment for the hymns, Mary looking serious with her straight rat's tail hair and her National Health glasses, John would read the lesson, and in turn we would all kneel in front of Mother to pray. Each prayer would start with the words of a hymn, converted by Mother into a prayer, which she hoped would convey to us the picture of Jesus that she saw, of a man who loved simplicity, truthfulness, the innocence of young minds, and who cared for us all. It started: 'Jesus once on Mummy's knee, was a little child like me. When I wake or go to sleep, lay thy hands upon my head. Let me feel thee very near, Jesus Christ, my Saviour dear. Be beside me in the light, be close by me through the night. Make me gentle, kind and true, do what I am bid to do. Help and cheer me when I cry, and forgive when I forget.' Then, with the introduction of: 'God bless Mummy and Daddy,' we could pray for whatever we liked, each one trying to outdo those who had gone before. We would pray for our friends, our relatives and our animals, for missionaries and natives, soldiers and sailors, nurses and doctors, lepers and lunatics, fishermen and farmers, exercising as we did so all our powers of invention and memory to introduce hitherto forgotten groups of people, preferably in desperate situations. As each new prayer progressed, so the plight of the soldiers and sailors became ever more hopeless, and the waves confronting the fishermen grew higher and higher. We would also hold a collection, and little sister Rachael and myself would argue and sometimes cry over whose turn it was to have the honour. Mother would give us all sixpence to put on the plate, which when collected, we would give back to her to put into the missionary box.

Father's upbringing had been much more liberal, coming under the influence of Methodism, the Church of England, and his odd collection of uncles and aunts, and he gave us the impression that his strict sabbath day observance was undertaken reluctantly. He nevertheless readily accepted most of the nonconformist doctrines inherited by Mother, expressing doubt about infant baptism and the pomp and circumstance of the Established Church, which he hoped, put him in a similar theological position to that of his historical hero, Cromwell.

The chapel itself had been built in 1894, but groups of believers had met in the village for a long time before. Throughout the area the nonconformist cause was quite strong, and ringing Cambridge were several small chapels, established during the time when dissenters had been prevented by law from preaching their version of the Bible within five miles of any borough. Indeed, it could have been claimed that the whole Baptist movement started in the nonconformist chapels of Cambridgeshire, for in a small village just to the north of the town, Charles Haddon Spurgeon had taken up his first church in the 1800s; much earlier still, the parson of the neighbouring village had fled to Holland where he became a leading Anabaptist. Somehow his heresies and debaucheries still seemed to linger on in the distant memories of High Churchmen, and they tended to regard chapel people as being slightly disreputable, even immoral.

I was not fond of going to chapel, as to me most of the sermons were boring, and I would usually fidget or sleep. Even some of the adults found it difficult to stay awake during the afternoon services, and with feelings of drowsiness growing from full stomachs and after-dinner snoozes, heads would gradually drop forward and there would be an occasional snore and the false teeth of one old man, dozing open-mouthed, would often fall together with a loud click.

The inside of the chapel was drab and if emptied of its furnishings and fittings it would have appeared more like a barn than a House of God. The floor was of bare boards, the ceiling was wooden, with large regular crossbeams, riddled with woodworm, and there were two rows of varnished benches, pompously called pews, but nothing like the real thing; they each held four people comfortably, and five at a squash, and one of the few concessions to comfort was the back rest on every pew, which gave only a minimum of support.

As each sermon wore on, so the pews seemed to get harder, as if the earlier dissenters had believed that austerity and arrant discomfort were conducive to sincere worship. The only other compromise to comfort was an old Tortoise stove at the back which when full of smouldering coke, was, as its makers suggested, 'slow but sure'. During cold winter afternoons its slowness would lead to buttoned up coats and shivering bodies, but by evening it would be throwing out such a heat, that those foolish enough to sit near it would be forced to shed their coats or to move as far away as possible.

A wooden pulpit was at the front, with a rail on each side, so that those who were carried away by their own oratory could stride up and down in safety; on the lectern was a large old Bible, with Roman numerals, and on the wall behind was a text in ancient script: 'I am the light of the world.' At each service there would be hymn singing, and preachers would urge the faithful to 'make a joyful noise unto the Lord', and sing four or five Sankey hymns. (An old hymn book containing over a thousand 'evangelical' hymns.) The sparse congregation would sing loudly but slowly, with all the gusto of a funeral dirge, and to anyone passing outside it must have sounded a most melancholy noise. The hymns themselves were usually morbid, with badly rhyming lines about blood, repentance, and the slain 'lamb of God'. One contained lines asking to be 'washed in the blood', but despite their goriness, they would often bring tears to the eyes of older members of the congregation.

The joyful noise was accompanied by Gordon, on the organ, a self-taught pianist who struggled manfully with a collection of knobs and keys that even the most accomplished musician would have found difficult. His task was made harder still by the fact that the contraption was powered by foot bellows that had to be pedalled vigorously. On special occasions, when the singing was more lively than usual, the whole organ and the vase of flowers balanced precariously on it, would shake wildly, and for Gordon the service would become something of an athletic exercise, rather than an act of worship.

Our minister had four chapels under his supervision, three in neighbouring villages, which meant that three-quarters of our services were conducted by local preachers. The form of each service was monotonously predictable, a hymn sandwich, consisting of a hymn, a reading, a hymn, a prayer, like a miniature sermon, another reading, another hymn, the real sermon, the final hymn, and the benediction. Halfway through, there would be a pause for the notices and collection, which brought welcome relief. When he was not milking, Father read the notices, being secretary, and would sometimes run into difficulties at the illegibility of his own notes. On one occasion when he looked up smiling, trying to decipher his handwriting, he was surprised to see several members of the congregation trying to suppress smiles of their own; it was not until he arrived home that he was told that his fly buttons were undone. After the notices the old village roadman, who sat in a pew with his wife and ancient father, took up the collection. He would plod to the front to get the collection plate, and then walk to the back, deliberately and slowly, just as if he was walking along one of his roads, with a plate instead of a wheelbarrow and broom; his head always bent slightly forward, an icicle usually on the end of his nose, and his feet splayed out at such an angle that if they had been the hands of a clock the time would have been just after a quarter to three. He was a familiar figure about the village, sweeping methodically, scything the roadside verges, sprinkling ice-covered corners with grit, and taking long, frequent rests leaning on his shovel, watching the world go by. Every Saturday evening he would come to our house just as *Dixon of Dock Green* was starting on the television, to collect the money for the village sick club, and he would finish his business just as *Dixon of Dock Green* ended. *Dixon of Dock Green* was first transmitted on 9th July, 1955 and sick clubs flourished until well after 1948 – when the better benefits of the Welfare State gradually started to replace them. His work would be done on the living-room table, with alternate glances to the television set and his small account book, and I would sit watching both the television and his icicle, to see whether he would sniff, or whether it would drip.

There was a great variety of preachers of all shapes, sizes and conditions, but all were convinced that they had been ordained by God to spread 'His Word'. There were anaemic clerks in smart suits, from the town, quiet yet earnest; tanned countrymen with broad rural accents, whose burning faith shone from them like braziers in the night; pale and spotty undergraduates, full of knowledge and quotations; and shouting Bible punchers, prophesying imminent doom. These last individuals would warn of hell and damnation, stride up and down, grip the wooden rail in anguish, thump the lectern with clenched fists, hold the Bible aloft for all to see, turn scarlet from their exertions, remind their listeners of the cross and spilt blood, and generally try to cajole the entire congregation into the Kingdom of God.

Men of high learning would express beliefs of the utmost simplicity, and others with little formal education would show a depth of understanding and intellect far above their stations. A university doctor, tall, pallid, and gaunt, condemned the practice of cremation, and expected to rise from the grave on Judgement Day, completely reassembled, while old Mr Carter, a toothless jovial widower with a blotched dark suit, a high wing-collared shirt, and poor eyesight, had an understanding that went far further than his appearance suggested.

Although most of the services followed a similar pattern there were many surprises. On one occasion an old preacher broke down with grief in the middle of his sermon and explained that his wife had recently 'passed on'. The next time he came, he again lost control, but explained that his tears were of joy, for he had just remarried. Another elderly man who gained my admiration told of how good God had been to him, yet as a young man he had fallen into a reaper and lost one arm and several fingers. A thatcher, who informed us that he had once been a drunkard and a thoroughly worthless individual, also preached occasionally. His ability to hold our attention did not come solely from his oratory, but also from his accent and appearance. During the week he wore a cap, and on top of his ladder his face had become weathered and brown. Once inside the House of God however, he took off his cap, revealing a large bald patch that seemed to stand out from its bronzed surroundings and reflect light. During his sermons he would talk of the disciples 'who were a goin' to see their master', of preaching trips he had made to the nearby mental hospital, 'the house on the hill', and of changes that he thought were being engineered by the Devil, 'entertainment, and these here motorcars that go around the corners so bloomin' fast, the drivers find themselves in eternity.'

One thing all the preachers insisted upon was that throughout their sermons and long extemporary prayers, full of exhortations, platitudes and cliches, it was not they who were speaking, but 'the Lord'; they were merely his willing vehicles. It was surprising therefore, that one Sunday a preacher announced at the beginning of the service that the Lord had not given him a message, and the whole hour was spent singing hymns. On another occasion a local evangelist called for a time of private prayer. To aid his own devotions he sat down in the pulpit, as for some reason Baptists usually sit down to pray. Minutes passed by in silence, until at last even the most senior members of the congregation became restless, it was then discovered that the preacher had fallen asleep; presumably the Lord needed a rest.

But services and sermons were not all boring or amusing, for occasionally the message passed on would be considered by some to be downright wicked. The atmosphere would become icy, and the preacher might even be interrupted while still in full flow. It happened once, when a young undergraduate was lecturing rather than preaching, and giving the impression that he had come to impart some of his knowledge to ignorant country folk. An old retired builder and his son, himself a local preacher, looked distinctly angry and then, when we were hearing how Jonah had not really been swallowed by a whale, pandemonium broke loose. There were cries of 'shame', 'it's the voice of the Devil', 'preach the gospel', and the old man stood up and began to gesticulate and argue. Mother was so distressed at the irreverent scene, that she ushered us out of chapel and took us home, leaving the battle still raging.

A pentecostal pastor also came to preach each year, and he saw it as part of his duty to actively search for new souls. Nearly all of his sermons ended with an appeal for the newly-saved to go forward, or to raise a hand during the final prayer; nobody ever responded, but he never gave up trying. Unfortunately, his delivery was such that even as small children we found it difficult to look at him, or listen, for any length of time for fear of laughing. Services taken by him were spent nudging one another, giggling, and fighting off bouts of more open laughter that would wither under Mother's reproachful glare. The trouble was that he was short and bald, he spoke extremely quickly and he punctuated all he said with nervous coughs and shouts of 'hallelujah', and 'God be praised'. To illustrate the power of God's word, he once told what he described as a true story, which we found particularly difficult to sit through: 'One day (cough cough), there was a man in London (cough cough), who hated the word of God (cough cough). Because of this (cough cough), he went into the House of God (cough cough), with his fingers in both his ears (cough cough). Fortunately (cough cough), he was bald (cough cough), and a fly settled on his bald pate (cough cough). He took his fingers out of an ear to swat the fly (cough cough), and the word of the Lord dropped in (cough cough). Doesn't the Lord work in a mysterious way (cough cough), Hallelujah (cough cough), praise His Name.'

After one afternoon service he was invited home for tea, and his effort to win souls continued in the drawing room. He asked both Mary and John if they were saved, they replied in the affirmative and were allowed to sit in front of the fire. He then asked Rachael and myself; I was embarrassed and mumbled that I did not know, and Rachael aged only five, could not understand him. Because of this we both had to kneel in front of him as he prayed over us, begging that we should repent of our sins and come to know the Lord. I was puzzled and indignant, Rachael was bewildered and upset, Mary and John sat sniggering, thinking the whole episode a huge joke.

Grandmother was a great admirer of village preachers, and had brothers and cousins who travelled round every Sunday trying to spread God's kingdom on earth, and she believed that it was the duty of all those who were able, to climb into a pulpit and speak, as often as possible. She was also sure that God helped and protected those who undertook his work, and told a story of her grandfather's cousin, to prove the point. The incident occurred when the family was still living out in the Fens, and the distant cousin had been a preacher, proclaiming salvation for the saved, and warning of fire and brimstone for all sinners. Because of this he made many friends, but he also made some enemies. One dark wintry night, when the Fen was at its most inhospitable, a man decided to lay in wait, by the side of a remote cart track, to murder him. After his preaching appointment had been duly fulfilled, the cousin returned home, passing the spot where the mischief was to take place. Nothing happened, for he was seen walking in the company of another man. Later the would-be killer repented and told of his evil intent, only to discover that the preacher had been with nobody that particular night, and had passed by alone.

Despite the influence of the church and chapel, it was still felt by some that God's presence was not real enough to non-believers, and if they would not go to God, God had to be taken to them. This was done by means of open-air services held in the High Street, or at the end of the Leys; the civil servant with the motor scooter played an accordion, old Mr Carter produced a violin, and there would be the usual hymns, prayers and sermon. The 'Word' would be specifically aimed at 'any of you listening at your windows, you can be saved. Repent and turn to the Lord.' Rarely was anybody seen listening, Father was extremely sceptical about the whole thing, and when it became apparent that a Wesleyan type revival was not going to rage through the village, the services gradually died out.

Outsiders sometimes appeared on the scene to help God with his work, door to door evangelists with brief-cases and pamphlets, and occasionally a missioner would set up a small tent with placards outside: 'Hear ye the Lord', or urging repentance; parents did not mind him coming, for it enabled them to send their children out in the evening, knowing that they would be kept from mischief. The missioner would fervently tell of God's goodness, but he also warned of the Devil, who, he said, spent his time trying to lead people astray, getting them to smoke, swear, and go into pubs, and whose subtle devices and fiendish stratagems could lure the unsuspecting away from the straight and narrow.

Uncle Jim has been both a missioner and a village preacher, and was continually on his guard against Satan, even when he paid visits to us at the farm. The first time he came into the living-room when the television set was on, he hustled his three children out, until it was switched off, to protect them from what he considered to be the work of the Devil. He was an unusual man, full of ideas for evangelising the world, before the Gadarene rush, which he saw gaining momentum, developed into a blind stampede of self destruction; but his ideas were rarely accompanied by a clear vision of how success could be achieved.

Mother's only sister had married him when he was a farmer as well as a part-time missioner, and he had a reputation locally for being a fiery man of God. He was short and stocky, like a working farmer, but his face was full of an earnest evangelical zeal that made him look prophetic and intense; his hair was greying and easily dishevelled, and his penetrating eyes viewed all wickedness from beneath bushy brows, like flashing orbs below miniature haloes of hair. He had inherited his farm from his father, but believed that God had called him for more important work; consequently he had sold the land and property to acquire some capital, and had bought a large mock Georgian country house in Essex. There, among its endless corridors and countless rooms, he hoped to establish a conference centre, from which a new Christian crusade would grow.

We were never too happy when he came to visit us, for he always seemed to be searching for some undesirable influence from which to protect us, or would detect a flaw in our characters that he would feel obliged to point out to Mother or Father. But we enjoyed visiting him, for his new house, with its many rooms, and the grounds, with their lakes, woods and gardens, made it the sort of place that most children dream about and there, with a modicum of invention, our normal childhood fantasies could be made almost real. The walls of the house were tall and white, of simple brick, and inside there were rooms with high ceilings and large fireplaces, others with small windows and an uncanny silence, there were great old chairs, a tiger skin rug with wide open jaws, swords, an enormous gong, and on the roof was a lightening conductor, bearing the scorch marks of innumerable storms.

The place also had other things, so Uncle Jim told us, for not only did he believe in God, but also in ghosts, and the house was said to be haunted. Indeed the routine of the conference centre was rarely interrupted by visitors, with the result that Uncle Jim seemed to have a great deal of spare time. Some of this he spent, with a new threshing machine, on neighbouring farms, but he also spent it trying to photograph ghosts. On one occasion he claimed to have been successful, but to me the picture seemed to be merely of a shaft of light shining through an open doorway. Regardless of the ghosts, strict religious observance was maintained when we were there, with prayers every morning, and grace at every meal. One day a real missionary arrived, a friend of Uncle Jim's, to show us lantern slides of his pioneer work in Peru.

In the grounds were several outbuildings, one with a loft and ladder that from day to day could be transformed into a spaceship or a submarine; a south facing wall where there were peach trees, figs, and vines, pleasantly intruding like part of a foreign land, and there were grass meadows down to a spinney, in which wild foxgloves grew and where grass snakes slithered over fallen leaves, or basked in the sun. There were the lakes too, which attracted us more than all the other things, for there, in a small rowing boat, we could become explorers, Indians, or oarsmen in the Oxford and Cambridge boat race. They also gave us another pastime, when Uncle Jim was out, for we would

drive stray hens down into the water, and watch them swim and float. With their feathers ruffled and their unwebbed feet being virtually useless as directional aids, they would drift about helplessly until blown to the shore.

Although the formal services at chapel were often an anaesthetising ordeal, there were special services that we did enjoy, and actually looked forward to. The best was undoubtedly the harvest festival, when the once a year worshippers would help to pack the pews, and the chapel's drabness was

61

transformed by bunches of freshly picked flowers; the fragrance of garden and field would mingle in the sacred atmosphere, together with a genuine feeling of thanksgiving that the harvest had again been safely gathered in. Flowers would bedeck the windows and pulpit, attracting peacock and tortoiseshell butterflies, fruit and vegetables always overflowed onto the floor from a trestled table at the front, the window sills were lined with large, tempting apples and, surprisingly, there would even be strings of flowering hops trailing over the clock.

Father gave sheaves of oats, barley and wheat, Mother cut the best bunches of grapes from the old vines in the greenhouse, Bert the postman usually sent along a special loaf baked in the shape of a basket containing the five loaves and two fishes, and there would be apples, tomatoes,  carrots and vegetable marrows in plenty. Even the old folk with overgrown gardens, would give packets of tea or sugar as their token of thanks. The traditional hymns were sung with a new-found verve and the preacher would deliver his sermon surrounded by flowers and asparagus fern. Feelings of happiness, celebration and relief permeated the building and made a welcome change from the solemnity and dreary incantations of a normal service. The evening after, the produce was auctioned off for money and Mother would buy us each an enormous apple or, as a special treat, a packet of jelly, some of which we were allowed to eat raw.

Christmas and Easter Day were the other occasions when it really did feel as if God was in chapel with us; in stark contrast to the normal Sundays when it seemed that if he was there, he must have been dozing in a corner like I often did. Easter morning was always greeted with an exchange of Easter eggs at the breakfast table, and then, as at Christmas, the goodwill seemed to spill over into the chapel. For us, Christmas always started early with Rachael and Mother having birthdays in mid-December, and John celebrating his on Christmas

Eve; the season of jellies, trifles, mince pies and crackers began on that day and, with carols from Kings College Chapel wafting from the wireless, the excitement gradually built up for the annual visit of Father Christmas. Every year, without fail, he deposited a stocking full of nuts, small toys, chocolates, and an orange on each bed, together with a larger present, a football, or a pair of roller skates, and each year until I was twelve, despite growing doubts, I lay feigning sleep as the great man tiptoed into my bedroom at about the time Mother and Father usually went to bed. Some years Phyllis, a lonely hairdresser befriended by Mother, who had grown into an aunt, came to stay, and in one stocking I found a used handkerchief just like hers, but still Father Christmas remained a reality. It was a time of laughter, eating, playing games and singing carols. In chapel, a decorated Christmas tree would sometimes appear; a practice that Father never failed to remind us, had pagan origins. He also threatened on a number of occasions to spend Christmas in the barn, because, he insisted, the true meaning of the birth of Jesus was being lost in a rush of shopping expeditions, tinsel, and sheer self-indulgence. He never carried out his threat, however, and always opened his presents with as much enthusiasm as everybody else.

As well as the special services we had no real objection to Sunday School either, and quite liked singing choruses and hearing Bible stories told in a language that we could understand. There were also certain inducements to go; an anniversary service in which we had to sit at the front and recite poems and sing hymns, but after which there was a prize giving, the size of the prize being dependent upon the regularity of attendance. There was a scripture examination which it was virtually impossible to fail, a chapel tea on Easter Monday, and an annual Sunday School outing. While petrol was still in short supply, this took the form of a picnic and games in one of Father's meadows, but later, as petrol became more plentiful, a coach was hired and we would all clamber aboard for a trip to Epping Forest or Whipsnade Zoo. Shortly before Christmas, the Sunday School party would be held, an event at which gluttony went unpunished, party games such as musical parcel and musical chairs were played, with sweets as prizes, and as the grand finale, Gordon would desert an old piano, on which he had accompanied the musical games, to show silent cartoon films which amused children and adults alike. Each year the film most eagerly awaited featured Donald Duck, an unscrupulous bandit, and a runaway circular saw.

Sunday School was considered to be so essential for us that each autumn a sale of work was held in the village institute to raise money for a new schoolroom. All the ladies of the chapel gave jars of chutney or jam, fruitcakes and tarts, embroidery and jumble to sell, and there would be a bran tub, and bagatelle played for a prize. Nobody ever dared to suggest a draw, for that too would have been classified as the 'work of the Devil'; gambling was something the chapel frowned upon, and the church permitted. However, the sale was popular with both chapel and church people, enabling them to meet for a chat as well as a bargain.

On a sunny day in 1952, the years of work were rewarded and the newly built Sunday School room was opened. It was small, with an adjoining kitchen and bucket lavatory, but it showed progress and demonstrated how God answered prayer. When we moved into the new room we found that Sunday School was vastly different from that held in the chapel, for we could see out of the windows, across the road, and into the bedroom windows of the old bakery. Mr and Mrs Creek did not live there alone, but had with them a middle-aged and mentally disturbed relation. This we found very amusing, as did many villagers, and although Mother informed us that he could not help his strange ways and that we should feel sorry for him, we eagerly kept watch, hoping that he had not been taken away in the little hospital van, reputedly yellow, to the 'looney bin'.

When he was home, halfway through Sunday School, the back of his hairless head would gradually appear in one of the windows for no explicable reason. As a result, we eagerly awaited this strange unnatural phenomenon and would sit expecting 'the moon to rise' at any minute. When it did, a tide of uncontrollable laughter would engulf us, which at times nearly drove our tall reserved teacher, Freda, to tears and inevitably acted as a catalyst for even more irreverent and rowdy behaviour.

The year after the new Sunday School room was opened, another long-awaited and prayed-for event took place; the opening of the baptistry. It should be, so we were told, the wish of every true believer, 'to have their sins washed away in the waters of baptism'. Baptism by total immersion was the doctrine of believers, and it made the gulf between the infant sprinkling of the church and the adult ducking of the chapel an irreconcilable one. As work on the baptistry progressed Rachael and myself often looked in on the workmen on our way to or from school and saw the hole of thick damp clay in front of the pulpit become tiled and fitted with a wooden top, until it was at last ready for the first batch of baptisms.

Hardly any member of the congregation had been baptised, and an air of expectancy built up as the date for the opening service drew near; we children were excited at the prospect of the forthcoming spectacle, and the older members thankful that one of the fundamental tenets of their belief could now be put into practice. The lid was removed, the baptistry was filled with water making it like a miniature swimming pool, a special water heater was submerged, and everything was ready. The chapel was packed on the appointed day, with the faithful and the faithless, those drawn by firm conviction and natural curiosity. As the minister in his waterproof suit walked slowly down the steps, and stood with the water lapping his waist, all watched intently as the first to be baptised followed him. After a short prayer, with his hands held together on his chest, he was suddenly plunged backwards beneath the surface, before he clambered out and staggered, streaming with water into the schoolroom.

The men all entered the water wearing their old clothes, but the women wore long white dresses with weighted hems at the bottom to preserve their modesty. One of the first ladies forgot to check her weights, and as she descended into the water, so her dress billowed up around her, much to our great enjoyment and her consternation. As each one went under, the children craned their necks to get a better view, while tears welled up into the eyes of the elderly who broke into a spontaneous rendering of the hymn: 'Oh Jesus I have promised, to serve Thee to the end,' heavy with emotion and thankfulness. It demonstrated to them that after nearly 2,000 years of Christianity, God was still at work in the villages.

CHAPTER 4

Sex and Violence

———

Although God could not actually be seen in person anywhere in the village, it was accepted by us that he was completely good, yet, at the same time, sex, the results of which could be seen everywhere, was considered to be thoroughly bad. This attitude again stemmed from Mother's puritanical ancestors who had been prim and prude and considered sex to be a taboo subject, never to be mentioned in front of the children. To them, nakedness was disgusting, the normal functioning of the body an embarrassment, and sexual desire an unforgivable sin unless carried out by Christian couples prayerfully, as if for the Lord.

Many generations before, Mother's family had lived in Scotland where their sexual ethics were in close affinity with those of many pious crofters who were said to remove all their cockerels from the hen runs on Sundays to prevent copulation on the Lord's Day. As it was, Mother grew up never properly learning the facts of life, with the whole emphasis of her early education being on how to prepare the spirit for death. Once, while exploring the farmyard on which she spent her childhood, she was sternly reprimanded by her father for watching a cow calve, and was sent to the house in disgrace. She was never told the correct names for certain parts of the body, and even after she married and produced a family, 'pregnant' was considered to be a dirty word.

By the time Mother came to answer our enquiries, while supervising our baths, she still did not know all the proper answers and had doubts as to just what children should know. Consequently, as John and I grew up we discovered that we had arms and legs, hands and feet, the same as everybody else, but we also each had a winky and a mary, and whenever anybody was going to have a baby, Mother informed us that they were expecting a happy event. It was not until

I was ten that I discovered most of the answers, and could by then get them confirmed by John who had gone to a grammar school and become a self-appointed expert on such matters.

I first heard a different name for my winky in the school playground, when a friend fell over and struggled to his feet clutching his groin in obvious pain.

'What's the matter?' I asked with concern.

'I've hurt my penis,' he replied with difficulty.

'What!' I asked, perplexed, 'What's that?'

'My penis,' he replied again, incredulously, by now massaging between his legs vigorously.

'That's not your penis,' I asserted imperiously, 'that's your winky.'

He quickly recovered: 'There's no such thing as a winky, my mum says it's a penis.'

'Well your mum doesn't know what she is talking about, 'cause my mum told me and my brother that we've both got winkies.' As far as I was concerned I had won the argument decisively; Mother couldn't be wrong. It was with some surprise that later I discovered that my winky really was my penis, my mary was my navel, and to make matters worse, Father Christmas was really Mother.

Despite Mother's apparent innocence, her relationship with Father was always warm and loving. We never heard them argue, they would often walk over the fields, arm in arm, nearly every day after dinner they embraced while leaning against the Aga, Mother would sometimes watch television from Father's lap, and of course, they produced four children without any difficulty or embarrassment. The sexual activity on the farm was accepted by both of them as part of the natural process, often an amusing one, and I watched all these things and wondered.

From a very early age it was clear that something not altogether straightforward was going on and that the difference between the girls and boys at school, and the ducks and drakes, the cows and bull, the goose and gander round the farm was not merely coincidental. When Rachael was expected and Mother's stomach got larger, still expecting a happy event and never 'pregnant', her condition was attributed to an answered prayer; God had decided to let us have another sister or brother.

But still doubts remained, for whereas the sows had rows of teats which their young would suck and bite greedily to get milk, the boar had two things in what we called his handbag, between his back legs, and the bull had an even larger and more pendulous one, and it seemed to me that these things must be for a purpose; the whole situation was one of mystery. My suspicions grew, particularly in the spring, when some most peculiar things would happen. On the pea sticks and the washing line male sparrows would flutter on top of female sparrows and appear to hit them with their tails. The bantam cockerels would fight each other and pursue the hens all over the garden, finally catching them and walking all over them. But the strangest performance of all came from the drakes who, in early spring, just before we found clutches of eggs hidden beneath masses of down, would behave in a most belligerent and bullying way. Their faces would become a deep red, their plumage would be immaculate, glistening with the health of natural oil, and they would strut past the ducks, their heads moving backward and forwards as if driven by clockwork, making guttural hissing noises, which to them must have been the erotic whispers of seduction. When a drake found a duck on her own he would chase her, seize her at the back of the head with his bill, clamber on top of her, tread clumsily up and down and wag his tail from side to side. Gradually the tail wagging and treading would build up to fever pitch, only to subside suddenly, with the drake sliding to the ground exhausted. The duck never seemed to run off after her unexpected release, as common sense suggested she should, but would flap her wings, rearrange her ruffled feathers, wag

her tail, and look as if she had enjoyed the whole procedure. Several times I chased a treading drake away, thinking that a fight was in progress, but Father would say, 'leave them alone, they're only play-ing'; it seemed to me a most unusual way to play.

Part of the mystery was lifted when we all went to spend a day at Gills Hill. The morning was sunny and Uncle Cyril told Father that he had to get a cow in calf, and so Father, John and myself accompa-nied him to a yard in which a young heifer stood. I expected that somehow Uncle Cyril would get this heifer to produce a calf on the spot, but instead two of his men went to a nearby shed and brought out a large, pugnacious-looking bull which they led by a pole attached to a ring through the end of the animal's nose. The yard gate was opened, the bull was released inside, and the men leant on the fence while Uncle Cyril sat on the gate, watching to see what

happened. The bull sniffed at the heifer's tail, he started breathing heavily, he looked very ill at ease and one of the men started to chuckle and shouted, 'come on get on with it'. Then, to my embarrassment, the bull's winky began to change, for out of his hairy sheath, a glistening pink carrot shaped thing kept slithering and disappearing back inside. As the bull became more agitated and interested in the heifer's hind quarters, so this strange winky slithered backwards and forwards more quickly, and then suddenly the bull reared up on his back legs and the winky plunged into the hole from which 'cow pancakes' usually came. The heifer's back legs bowed, the bull's front legs were over her back, and his own back legs trembled as he blew and thrusted. At the same time, Uncle Cyril scrambled from the gate muttering in alarm; 'Oh no, he's gone up the wrong hole', and much to my amazement on this morning of surprises, he ran to the bull, seized its winky in both hands, took it from one hole, and with some difficulty inserted it into the lower one out of which I knew calves emerged.

Father and the men were greatly amused and strange comments continued until the bull finally returned to all fours, breathing hard and exhausted. 'We'll just have to see what sort of a calf she has now, won't we?' Uncle Cyril said with relief, and it gradually dawned on me while the bull and heifer stood next to one another, quiet and content, that it was this strange and rude ritual that somehow manufactured babies, whether cows, pigs or people.

After this, when I saw the animals playing their special sort of game, I would often stand and stare, especially when it involved the boar and one of his collection of loose-living sows, for we considered his behaviour to be thoroughly disgusting, yet took a childish delight in watching it. Everything we knew to be wrong in human behaviour, he did with his mistresses; he sniffed at the favoured sow in all sorts of places, he would rub his nose up and down her teats in ecstasy, and if the sow passed water he would drink it with relish. 'Cor I bet that tastes good,' Charlie would say if he, too, was watching. Finally, after a steady build up of excitement the boar would mount his sow, but even then he would take many minutes to complete his duty and always seemed to have the most brazen self-satisfied leer on his face.

Before the revelations at Gills Hill, girl friends had been thought

70

by me, as well as by most of my friends, to be decidedly cissy and when Mother had gone into a nursing home to have Rachael, the interest I took in the naked daughter of the lady who looked after us as she was bathed in a papier-mâché bath tub in front of the fire, was purely academic. Afterwards, however, although girls were always considered to be a nuisance and spoilsports, the idea of a girl friend was not so outrageous as it had earlier been.

The first feelings of what I took to be real love developed so quickly that I was surprised by them. They came upon me when a girl a year older than I, who was due to take her eleven plus examination, arrived at school carrying a large box. Her father, who was serving with the RAF in Hong Kong, had sent it to her, and inside was a new dress which our teacher let her put on to show the class. It was a Chinese kimono, that shone with a pure silken sheen of delicate pink, and which to me seemed to match the colour of her country cheeks. She looked beautiful. Each time I saw her after that my heart fluttered, yet somehow she seemed unobtainable.

Everything changed one morning during an arithmetic class, when a craze of writing love letters was in progress. With heads down over sum books as if struggling with immensely difficult problems, letters declaring love and devotion were being written on scraps of paper and furtively passed from desk to desk, until they reached their correct destinations. I wrote one to the girl who had become my vision of perfection, telling her that I loved her, and covering the paper with kisses. Soon a scribbled note came back saying that she loved me, too, and I could hardly wait for school to end.

In the afternoon, desks were cleared to one side and the puppet stage was pushed out for a full rehearsal of Aladdin which we were shortly due to perform in front of another school. The teachers and those too young or unreliable to take part sat at the front, the puppeteers were out of sight at the back. The performance started, and soon the emperor, with me manipulating the strings from above, strode on to meet Widow Twankey who was worked by my new-found love. Still flushed with the excitement of our notes we moved much closer than was necessary, as did the emperor and Widow Twankey below. I put my free arm around her waist and as she looked invitingly and knowingly at me, I kissed her smiling lips.

'What's going on behind there?' screamed Mrs Munden, our teacher, startling us. My emperor had taken off and was suspended in mid-air.

The seeds of love were sown, and several times after school we would walk together hand in hand, or arm in arm, as I had seen Mother and Father do, or we would sit in the long grass on the Leys, talking, picking buttercups and kissing. Our favourite place was in a small clump of bushes and brambles at the side of the Leys, which we could enter, and where we could kiss and entwine our arms with no danger of being seen.

Elsewhere, some younger children were discovering each other in a much more clinical fashion, without the spark of romance that I felt guiding me. As we went in one direction, they went in another, across the recreation ground, over a ditch, finally disappearing into a small, overgrown spinney. There, skirts were lifted up, short trousers taken down, and visual inspections were made of each other's differences. One girl's *pièce de résistance* was to squat down and relieve herself as the boys looked on with eyes agog. It did not take long for rumours of these goings-on to reach the ears of parents, and a policeman visited most of the participants, warning them of what would happen if they did it again.

At about that time too, my romance foundered, for on meeting at our place in the brambles one afternoon, my girlfriend insisted that I did not really love her, but loved the fat girl I sat next to in class. I protested my innocence but she called me a 'bloody liar', and I turned round and wandered home; after all, I decided, I didn't really like her anyway.

Despite the fact that Mother had certain doubts about just how much we should know about conception, she had grown up to be considerably more liberal than her forebears and made no attempt to conceal from us the beauty and the tragedy of birth, for she saw each new life successfully started as part of God's continuous process of creation; a process of renewal – pure, and full of hope for the future. This we could understand and see in every new thing that entered consciousness; in the Muscovy ducklings as they emerged from their eggs, damp and perplexed, peering at their surroundings from behind a protective wall of down. Within a few hours of hatching,

their mother, with a look of pride
tempered with concern at her
new responsibilities, would lead
them, with head held high, into
the outside world, offering them
shelter beneath her wings when
it rained, and protection from
cats and carelessness that would
otherwise prey on their inno-
cence. The ducklings themselves were like small web-footed wisps of
brightly coloured down, black and yellow, paddling from puddle to
puddle and chasing insects in a sea of grass. We could see too, this
renewal of life in the boxes of tiny chickens that arrived at the station
every year, and which Father released, cheeping and inquisitive,
beneath a paraffin heated foster mother; in the litters of pigs, with
the piglets lying pink and peaceful, basking in the warmth and
security of their contentedly incumbent mother, and in the newly-
born calves as they tottered on unsteady legs, trying to walk.

It was watching the birth of a calf that really did fill us with wonder, with the struggle, the labour, and sometimes the pain, giving
way to new life, frail, inquiring, and covered with steam. First the
front legs would slowly appear, then the nose, and then after much
straining the head would gradually emerge; once this was clear, the
rest of the birth was usually quick, with the wet warm
body slipping to the ground and with a sudden gasp for air, the breath of life would
seem miraculously to enter; it was indeed
an inspiring process which often left me
watching the newly-born calf for hours
on end. Within minutes of birth, a quiet
maternal lowing would begin, far different from the usual vacuous and
meaningless moos, as if enquiring with
motherly concern if all was well. Then, as
if to reassure herself and her new-born
offspring, the cow, with long and
loving tongue, would lick the calf

73

as it lay there steaming, and looking round with large, blinking, and astonished eyes. Shortly afterwards, the struggle to stand and to gain basic balance began and once that had been achieved, the swaying calf would instinctively commence its search for food. Often it would look between its mother's front legs first, but always it turned eventually to the tight bulging udder, with its four teats full and sometimes dripping with bisnings.

After two or three days the calves were normally taken away from their mother and given milk, or a substitute made from powder, from a bucket. To get a new calf to put its head down into a bucket instead of up to where an udder should have been required much skill and patience. Father would encourage each fresh arrival to suck his fingers and then gradually lower its head into a bucket to drink, but even so the calf would often butt, as it had done against its mother's underside, to make the milk flow faster, and knuckles would be grazed on the bucket's side, hooves would tread on toes and, with particularly difficult learners, the bucket would be sent flying. Once the calf had become accustomed to the new method of feeding, Father would allow me to copy him and my fingers would become sticky with the calf's saliva and warm with the milk.

At the same time as we saw new life, we also saw the harshness and misery of death; in cold limp bodies, the still limbs, and the glazed eyes of those young animals that never took that first magical breath of vivification. The cycle of life and death was an inescapable part of living on a farm; it did not permit emotion, but created a high regard for life and an acceptance that death was both natural and inevitable. It also showed, in the ducklings encased in unyielding shell, or a calf ripped open by an angry horn, that it could be violent as well as ugly.

The saddest casualties were again the calves, for difficult calvings were common, when the front legs would show and the cow would strain and bellow in anguish, but nothing more would come. Father, Jim and sometimes the vet would tie a rope to the protruding legs, fix the other end to a length of wood and then heave and pull, forcing their heels into the ground, until the calf was dragged from its mother. Occasionally a calf would try to emerge sideways, or backwards, which meant an even harder labour, and Father would insert his arm to well above the elbow, and push and pull, trying to turn the calf into the correct position and even then, after such a struggle, the calf would often be dead.

One calf was so large that although trying to emerge the correct way, its head just would not break through. Eventually it became a matter of saving the cow herself and as Father and other willing hands held the cow, Jim pulled the calf out with a tractor; it was an enormous bull calf, but it lay glazed and dead, in a pool of blood and afterbirth. The cow clung on to life for several days, but the ordeal proved too much, and finally she gave up, put her head down to rest in the straw and died.

The unexpectedness of death and the transience of life were shown to us on many occasions. John saw a young calf put in with a foster mother, tossed to the roof and killed. During a gale Father tried to throw some baler wire on to a roof and out of the way, but the wind caught it, wound it round a live overhead electric cable, which snapped and came crashing to the ground. It wrapped itself around one of Father's best young heifers, the fuses did not blow, and it was electrocuted. And in the fields adjoining the brook a young bullock contracted black leg and was reduced to a hobble; one of its front legs became swollen, it frothed at the mouth, the vet pronounced it incurable and I watched with John and Father as the knacker drove to it in his lorry, put the bell-shaped humane killer between its eyes, struck the handle and the bullock's twitching body lay dead, with a bullet embedded in its brain. The knacker was remarkably jovial for one whose living was so grim, he winched the body into his lorry, and carted it away for dog meat.

Nearly every year some great mishap or fight for survival would take place. One winter's day the boar got out and fell into a large, almost bottomless ditch, full of black stinking mud, but ropes were put over him and he was hauled out just in time. A freshly calved cow collapsed with milk fever while walking through a morass of mud and had to be propped up with bales of straw and injected with calcium until she was well enough to stagger out herself.

The cows were Dairy Shorthorns, red or roan animals, quite stocky and all with short, sharp horns. Often, because of their butting, when confined to the yard during winter, there would be torn flesh to stitch, and at other times there would be udders torn by barbed wire to patch up and sew. As a result Father became extremely skilled in using cotton wool soaked in disinfectant, together with a needle and thread, to repair wounds that would otherwise have remained open and gaping and brought in enormous veterinary bills. Young pigs were especially vulnerable to ripping teeth if they wandered into a neighbouring sty, and Father successfully patched up some that looked to be quite hopeless cases. Occasionally a larger pig would damage itself, and if this happened, rather than letting it die and wasting it, Father, who still fancied himself as a part-time butcher, would help it on its way by slitting its throat and bleeding it so that it could be eaten. Where he normally washed the milk buckets he would pour scalding water over the carcass and scrub it to remove the bristles, and then the house would be transformed into a miniature butcher's shop. The body would be transferred to the kitchen table, and cut into a variety of joints and chops, and in the old dairy at the end of the house, a large greasy vat would be filled with a brine specially prepared to pickle hams. Little was wasted, with Mother making brawn from the trotters and head, and Father collecting all the odd bits and pieces to mix with seasoning and rusk, to make sausages from the old traditional family recipe; these tasted delicious, especially when compared with the sausages normally purchased during the time of rationing, for they seemed to be made mostly of bread crumbs.

On occasions, violence and the threat of injury or even death, spilled over from the animals to affect us. At its most mild it took the form of the goose and gander advancing in menacing fashion with heads down, hissing to protect their new brood of spruce and obedient goslings, or the broody hens scolding and pecking to preserve their eggs. Freshly calved cows were also unpredictable and could not tolerate dogs; normally, our labrador, Judy, would help to round up the cows for milking, and they would retreat before her barking and snapping teeth like a collection of cowardly matrons. But as soon as a calf was born, the bitch sensed a change of mood and would stay a respectful distance, for the new mother's timidity would be transformed innately into a mood of protective maternal bellicosity. When I was very small, a freshly calved cow suddenly ran at Judy and trampled all over me in the process as I happened to be standing directly between them. Father picked me up, bespattered with mud and cow dirt, crying, but unhurt.

Later there were numerous near misses, when serious injury was only just avoided, such as a day in late harvest when a cartload of straw toppled over while we were riding on top, but we came to no harm. Whatever season of the year it happened to be, one of our favourite pastimes, and that of our friends, was to ride on the trailers, climbing on and jumping off while they were in motion. Once, having jumped off a small two wheeled trailer, I experienced great difficulty in climbing back on. As the tractor proceeded to pull it along the road, I ran alongside and tried again, in front of one of the wheels where it was lower, but John, already safely aboard, tickled me under the arms and I fell to the ground. The trailer bumped, and I was left lying in the roadside, with the tyre's tread cut in blood and burning pain across my leg.

But the most worrying aspect of violence on the farm was Father's relationship with the bull as, for some inexplicable reason, a natural antipathy had built up between them. Father mistrusted the bull and tended to treat him with contempt, and the bull always looked at Father morosely, as if biding his time. The inevitable occurred one day when Father, Jim and Percy wanted to clear out the bull pen, a small barred enclosure in the corner of the covered yard. To get the bull out, Father had to enter the pen, grab the bull's chain which ran from a small head harness, down the front of his head and through a ring at the end of his nose. Father caught the chain in one hand and tried to open the gate with the other. This he did clumsily, and the bull seizing his opportunity, burst free and out of the pen, brushing Father aside. Once out, he swivelled with startling speed for his size and maliciously butted Father in the stomach, knocking him down and pinning him against the concrete surround of the bull pen manger and tried to rip into his stomach with a horn. Percy went white, his mouth dropped open, and he stood rooted to the spot as he watched with horror, while Jim rushed forward, as he had many years before in bayonet practice, with a four tined muck fork in his hands instead of a rifle, and thrust the points into the animal's shoulder until he hit bone.

The bull reluctantly backed off, and Percy was sent to get the bull pole. He returned, but still full of fear, failed to see that the catch had not clicked shut to secure the bull's ring to the pole. Jim put his weapon down, Percy relaxed, and Father bent and stretched to ensure that he was all right. The bull sensing that it was not tethered correctly shook its head, the catch released the ring and the animal knew that it was again free, with all three men caught quite unprepared and vulnerable. Percy's lower jaw dropped once more, but with adrenalin now pumping through his veins he turned and fled, scrambling over a fence and disappearing from view; Father ran towards the gate and Jim made for his fork. The bull could not have cared less about Percy or Jim, and again spun round and made for Father, who, just before reaching the safety of the gate, stumbled and fell. The bull, head down, hit him at full gallop in the middle of the back and

then began to kneel on him, trying at the same time to gore with its horns. Jim, remembering his old instructor's commands, 'twist it so that the guts come out,' charged again, and with an angry cry of 'Get back you bugger', plunged the tines between neck and shoulder with all his might, drawing blood and forcing the animal away. Father rolled clear under the gate, Percy was not to be seen and Jim was left facing the bull alone.

After helping tether the animal with a cart rope, Father staggered into the house, badly bruised and shaken, where Mother helped him to wash and put him to bed. Miraculously it seemed no serious damage was done, but from that time onwards he suffered from periodic back trouble.

Jim's advice was quite clear after this: 'I wouldn't have the bugger on the place if it were mine. I'd get a gun and put a bullet through its bloody head.' For once Father took most of his advice and shortly afterwards the bull was loaded up and taken away for slaughter. A younger and more docile animal followed, but Father finally yielded to pressure from Mother and that too was sent away. The bull's task was taken over by a man with ginger hair, who began to drive regularly into the farmyard with a case full of long glass tubes in the boot of his car. 'Cor, I bet they don't like them half as much,' was Charlie's comment when he first saw a tube inserted. We called the artificial inseminator 'the ginger headed bull'.

The realities of life and death also came to me in a much more unpleasant and personal way, for at about the age of three I developed asthma. Each winter, without fail, I would have weeks of wheezing and coughing and days of struggling for breath. There would be times when each new breath was a major effort and I would pray forlornly to Jesus who loved children that I should not be allowed to die. Every time I caught cold, with monotonous regularity bronchial asthma followed and my lungs would sound like a boiling cauldron, continually bubbling and wheezing. My whole chest felt tight, as if my ribs had fused together and could not expand, and each time I was engulfed by a deep hacking cough, my whole body shook and a rasping pain seared through my lungs and into my stomach. Mother would lay her hand, or a damp flannel, on my brow to soothe my burning forehead, and many times she slept wrapped in blankets on the floor of my bedroom, to be with me as I wheezed through the night.

If I got too bad the doctor was called, regardless of the time of day or night, and he always arrived quickly, uncomplaining, with a smile, words of comfort and reassurance, together with M and B tablets that I had to swallow, crushed in water, and taken from a teaspoon. He was young and considerate, he always had time to talk and listen, and his slight north country accent was warm and understanding; he was everything a family doctor should have been. He had recently arrived to run the practice temporarily, as he was newly married and wanted some security; Rachael had the distinction of being the first new baby to come into his care.

The aftermath of each bout of illness was extremely tedious. I had to be careful to prevent reinfection, Mother would keep saying 'wrap up well', making sure that I always wore my scarf outside, and I had to stop playing all running games until my wheeze had completely disappeared.

Once, despite the activities of the doctor and the M and B's I got steadily worse, my temperature soared and pneumonia set in. Wearing pyjamas and wrapped in a blanket, I sat on Mother's lap as Father drove us in to the hospital in Cambridge. It was Poppy Day, the Saturday before Remembrance Sunday, when the undergraduates sold paper poppies to raise money for the disabled service men of the two World Wars. On that day the town became chaotic, with road blocks, processions, decorated floats, and a complete breakdown in normal law and order. Both the townspeople and the undergraduates looked forward to the revels and the only people who showed signs of impatience were the drivers of cars and lorries who had hoped to pass quickly through the town.

Fortunately there were no queues in the early afternoon and Father scattered students at the only road block we encountered by driving straight through them, and he delivered me safely to hospital (the emergency admissions section is now

Browns Restaurant). In the forecourt pipers were marching up and down, wearing kilts and their special military regalia, playing for the benefit of patients as part of their Poppy Day activities. Normally Mother loved to hear the sound of bagpipes as they seemed to stir something in her ancestral memory, but it was my wheeze that commanded her attention on that day, and the ordered wheezes of the pipes went almost unnoticed.

In the antiseptic atmosphere of the children's ward I lay for several days, recovering sufficiently to fight violently when the hospital doctor called to take a sample of blood from my arm. In the ensuing struggle it required five pairs of hand to hold me down while the needle was inserted, and because of my resistance, a large bruise formed and covered a quarter of my arm; as a result the thought of giving blood horrifies me even to this day, bringing to mind the picture of an enormous needle and syringe, and I could never volunteer to be a blood donor.

The course of my asthma was entirely predictable; in the summer, under clear warm skies my lungs would heal themselves and fill with pure clear air, redolent with the scents of the season, and all would be well; but with the fogs of autumn, raw winter days, smoky chimneys, and the lingering damp of cold wet clay, they would become almost like sponges, trying to drown me in the liquids of my own rib cage.

Probably because of the mental and physical effort involved in fighting off my asthma, I also developed an uncontrollable temper that, when ignited, would lead me in rage to throw anything that came to hand and struggle stubbornly, and sometimes stupidly, regardless of the odds against me. After being discharged from hospital following the removal of my tonsils, I refused to talk to Mother and Father as I resented the way in which they had left me, and in any case, I was convinced that my tonsils had been left untouched. Cousin John, who still sometimes baited me, would be attacked with sticks or stones at the slightest provocation, and bricks, pitchforks, broken axe handles, unripe apples, chunks of ice and rotten eggs, all featured at some time as part of my armoury. Even brother John, who was stronger than me, would retreat rapidly when I was in this state.

When a friend of Mother's came to stay and had to look after us alone one evening, I decided that I did not want to go to bed at the appointed time and threw a pile of newspapers that had accumulated under the television table all round the living-room, finally locking myself in the bathroom. I bit the dentist when he wanted to remove the last loose remnant of my milk teeth and he got permission from Mother to manage me as best he could. They both manhandled me in the chair, and the tooth was finally removed long before I realised the fact.

Even when playing cricket on the lawn, an occasion we all looked forward to for both Mother and Father would join in, my temper would often lead to the game ending prematurely for me; whereas I liked fielding and bowling, I did not like being 'out' when batting, especially if I thought that my innings had been too short. As a result, if I had not been at the wicket very long and the bails were knocked off, or if John was to appeal for leg before wicket just to antagonise me, I cried, shouted, knocked the stumps out of the ground, threw the bat away, and did everything that in other circles would have been considered 'not cricket'. Mother and Father often took this view as well, and the only way they could restore peace was to send me indoors.

My temper also reaped its own harvest of trouble. One day, Chris, a boy who lived nearby and who I often fought on my way home from Sunday School, aroused my wrath so I threw a bucket of water over him. Later in the day he got his revenge by creeping up on me unawares and pushing me headlong into a clump of stinging nettles.

Normally, however, we, like the animals, lived in harmony, facing each new day as it came, with learning and experience merging into each other. As time passed, my temper gradually subsided, I surrendered the bat willingly when 'out' at cricket, Chris became a friend, and my first girl friend grew up and left the parish to search for true love elsewhere.

CHAPTER 5

The School

———

Just past the chapel a small path branched away from the High Street. This was Church Lane, along which all churchgoers had to walk, as well as most of the school children, among whom, after the age of four, I was numbered. Along one side of the lane was a high wooden fence, with the occasional knot hole through which we would peer without much success, trying to see the contents of the vicar's garden. This changed abruptly, after a few yards, to a brick wall of a similar height. On the other side of the path was a wooden cottage, divided down the middle to make two small semi-detached

homes. The strip of well-worn track then turned sharply left, at right angles, with the seemingly prison-like wall of the vicarage continuing on one side, and the much lower wall of the churchyard on the other. As the two walls again turned away from each other to encompass their respective occupants, the living and the dead, Church Lane ran into School Lane, across which stood the village school; the school house, the playground, and the school building itself, with its porch, its slate roof and neatly stacked pile of milk crates all separated from the road by an old wooden fence. This was the place where we, like most children in the neighbourhood, received our early formal education.

It was almost the quietest spot in the village; the only traffic being the horses and carts from a nearby farm, loaded in winter with steaming manure and in summer with great quantities of hay or straw. The occasional tractor also passed, as well as a few cars, usually containing travelling agricultural salesmen wanting to buy corn or sell pig food. School Lane came to a dead end at the farm, one of the oldest farms in the parish, with the remnants of an ancient moat on one side of the farmhouse, which was said by some to attract large eels that quickly turned the colour of the mud surrounding them and even in the frying pan they managed to retain its taste. By one side of the school was the village institute, wooden and creosoted, usually empty during the day except for the monthly meetings of the Over-Sixties, or the Women's Institute, and further along the road towards the 'planton' (plantation: a triangle of grass and trees in the middle of the road, at the confluence of School Lane, the High Street, and a road to another village), was the Hoops, usually quiet and empty until evening. The church, with its Norman tower of field stones and rubble, its graveyard full of mossy headstones, the moving shade and chill beneath its spreading horse-chestnuts and dark yews, and the vicarage with its windows, chimney stacks, and trees, standing above the encircling wall, dominated this part of the village and the school.

This was no mere coincidence, for the village school was also a church school, one in which the teachers were appointed by the school managers and the faith and Articles of the Established Church were unashamedly propagated. Every morning, once the Big Room had been reached, we stood behind our desks as our teacher began the day with 'Good morning children', and we would all reply in unison, 'Good morning Miss Whitmell.' After the register had been called, during which time nobody dared to doze for fear of Miss Whitmell's wrath if they failed to shout 'present' in response to their name, devotions began; the Lord's Prayer, together with prayers of intercession for those in the village who were ill or in need. Then came scripture, a Bible story which was sometimes acted, with over-enthusiastic robbers waylaying the traveller in the parable of the Good Samaritan, with horrifying acts of simulated savagery, or Jesus with great solemnity and dignity performing miracles, walking on water and healing lepers.

At the end of each day there were evening prayers, when we each put our chair on top of our desk and stood with heads down, hands together and eyes closed, as Miss Whitmell said her version of the prayer for evening, taken from the Book of Common Prayer: 'Lighten our darkness we ask thee O Lord,' she intoned, 'and by Thy great mercy defend us from all the perils and dangers of this night, till morning light appears. And may the grace of the Lord Jesus Christ, the love of God, and the help and comfort of the Holy Spirit be with us all this night and for evermore,' at this point we joined in with a loud 'Amen', eager to be let out and restored to freedom as quickly as possible. Only once was the quiet and orderliness of evening prayers interrupted – on hearing water splashing on the floor, eyes were furtively opened, and we glanced aghast at one small girl, in a mixture of surprise and disgust, for with her hands together and eyes closed, she stood wetting her knickers.

The morning sessions of R.I. often had their stormy periods, as everyone had to learn the Ten Commandments and the Creed off by heart, and those who forgot, or were slow, were liable to have Miss Whitmell's very considerable anger fall about their heads. Those of us who came from Baptist homes were lucky, our prayers on Sundays were extemporary, and some parents looked upon the incantations and responses of the Church of England in the same light as they viewed primitive witch doctors and tribesmen chanting before evil spirits, sacred mango trees, and green-eyed monsters. Consequently, while the others suffered considerable anguish trying to remember the strange phrases and words used by saintly scholars of an earlier age, Miss Whitmell was lenient with us, and when we failed to remember a commandment or a section of the Creed, her rebukes were mild and her anger remained in store for somebody else.

On Ascension Day the whole school had to attend church, as we all did later in the year for a special school harvest festival service, and there was no release then for those of us from heretical homes. The inside of the church was far different from that of the chapel, with the tower, nave and chancel containing an atmosphere which was quite unfamiliar to me, and when confronted by the mysteries of the Prayer Book, jumping from one page to another and kneeling on hard hassocks to pray, the services became almost completely incomprehensible.

The only thing that encouraged me to make an effort to follow these strange ways was my grandfather's name carved on one of the pews, which signified that he, like many others had bought a pew for the church when it had been refitted. It also showed something else, for it revealed just how far Father's theology had travelled; physically from one end of Church Lane to the other, but spiritually an immeasurable span.

A reputedly Saxon font stood at one end of the building, the altar at the other, and along the walls were a number of fading fourteenth century murals depicting strangely clad men, hunting, praying, and fighting. Beneath the high wooden beams of the roof and a great stone archway between the chancel and the nave, was an ancient wooden screen, the work of a craftsman long dead, with ornately carved spandrels and sweeps and curves of delicately foliated and trefoiled wood. The procession of choir and vicar passed through the central arch of the screen, and on either side there were rows of tiny arches, through which the stained glass

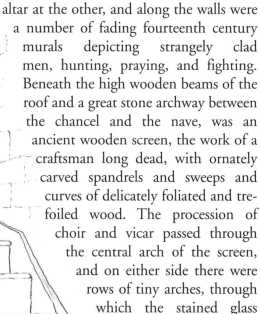

windows could be seen as distant areas of filtered light in an otherwise drab atmosphere. In front of the screen was a pulpit, again made of wood, hexagonal and far grander than the one in the chapel. It was entered by steps, and surrounded by wooden panels, enriched with simply carved diamonds and representations of other precious stones. Above it, to contain the sound, was a more intricately cut canopy, with wooden orbs pointing downwards at four corners; to me it looked like a great umbrella, with four large drips of wooden water about to fall to the ground, and it was beneath these that the vicar would preach.

We had to show all the necessary reverence and respect to the vicar, for he was the titular head of the church in the village, as well as the main overseer of the school. Whenever he crossed the playground and entered the classroom we all had to put our pencils down and stand up to greet him with: 'Good morning Vicar', and wait for his permission to sit down. Often he would appear from a doorway half way along the vicarage wall, cross Church Lane with two or three large strides, and disappear into the churchyard. With his black cassock trailing behind, almost like a pair of drooping wings, he looked from a distance like an ageing supernatural phantom, going to roost somewhere in the branches of a yew tree above the grave stones.

He was an elderly man, but even though his strength was gradually ebbing away he still tried to lead his faithful flock. One day our teachers led us out of school and into School Lane, where we stood in an orderly manner until the vicar was carried out of the vicarage on a stretcher and loaded into an ambulance; we all then waved good-bye vigorously. A slight smile forced itself across his cadaverous face as he raised a feeble arm, but I could not help feeing uneasy, equating his situation with that of Diamond and the cattle truck, being loaded up and taken away to die; nevertheless, I too, waved cheerfully.

The day the Bishop came to the village we again trooped out into School Lane, where we stood in awe as the great man arrived to bless the new churchyard gates; wearing his gold braided mitre, his ornately decorated vestments, and carrying his shepherd's crook, he seemed even holier than the vicar. The old white wooden gates had gone rotten and the new ones of wrought iron showed four golden keys, the keys of Heaven, thought to be appropriate for St Peter's church. As we watched the Bishop pray at the gates, and then walk slowly into the churchyard, followed by his entourage of cassocked clergymen in much less splendid robes, they looked rather like a gathering of elderly ladies in long dresses out for a country walk. I could not understand why St Peter needed four keys to admit people into Heaven, or why the Bishop dressed up almost like a woman.

Miss Whitmell, our headmistress had come to the school in 1945, and appeared to most parents as a charming little lady, living peacefully in the school house with her aged mother. She had greying hair, horn-rimmed glasses and thick stockings, which outwardly conveyed an image of respectability, refinement, and motherliness all at the same time. To her pupils however, she was something entirely different, for 'Ol' Ma Whitmell' was a teacher to be feared as well as respected. If she could not persuade knowledge into empty heads then her philosophy was to shake or shout it in, and as the neighbourhood was so quiet, visitors to the school could often hear her busily persuading well before they turned the corner in Church Lane. There were occasions when we would sit literally quaking with fear, seeing her as a great educational ogre, but as time went by her despotism was offset by periods of almost affectionate mildness, and it was clear even to the most timid that her teaching methods were not tyrannical for tyranny's sake, but based on a sincere desire to 'get us on'.

Mother refused to take me to school on my first morning, remembering her teaching days when the very presence of a parent at the school gate often induced a flood of tears from the child as well as arousing misgivings in the mother. Instead, in my new pair of short trousers, new to me that was, but handed down from my brother, and with my socks pulled up, I set off with John on the long walk to school. Mother gave me a piece of paper with my name and age clearly written on it and John had instructions to see that I arrived safely in the Little Room, before he went for the first time into the Big Room.

Sure enough, at the entrance to the playground just as Mother had anticipated, one new boy, loth to leave his mother, was screaming, his face contorted with grief. His mother lingered at the gate, not wanting to leave him in such a state of distress, and Mrs Munden the infant teacher was trying to calm him down, glancing at the mother, hoping that she would go away.

Punctually at 9 o'clock, Miss Whitmell rang a large hand bell from the porch steps and everybody filed into school, including the reluctant newcomer, and John quickly ushered me into the Little Room. It really was a little room, more like a store room than a class room, and described by one Ministry Inspector as 'the Black Hole'. The desks were clustered together in groups of four, there were shelves, wall charts and a large open fireplace with a high black guard. Mrs Munden, quite young and ebullient, with bright red lips, quickly settled over the class, rather like a broody hen with a family of newly hatched chicks; cooing, clucking, and reassuring. I gave her my piece of paper, and glancing at it briefly she said, 'Ah yes, I've had your brother and sister already haven't I?' and feeling that she was already a friend I obediently went to the desk allocated to me, where I had to sit next to a girl who lived close to the farm and who I did not like; when Mrs Munden was not looking I pulled her pigtails.

There were just over forty children at the school altogether, of whom about sixteen were in the Little Room. The enclosed atmosphere was generally happy, with a heavy fug quickly building up when the coal fire was burning, as well as a steady buzz of industry and activity. Every morning a calendar was operated, giving the date and a model of a woman in sunshine or a man in rain, depending on the weather, and then we had reading which we learnt phonetically by seeing each letter of the alphabet on a wall chart, and reading together: 'A for apple; B for bat; C for cat,' as each page was turned. We also learnt visually by recognising the shape of unusual words, such as 'elephant', which I could pick out long before I could construct it from individual letters. Tables were chanted rhythmically: 'Once two is two. Two twos are four. Three twos are six. Four twos are eight,' and if anybody's mind wandered Mrs Munden could shout almost as loudly as Miss Whitmell. Painting, plasticine modelling, and nature study; all this went on in the cramped surrounds in a state of orderly chaos until last thing in the afternoon, when all became quiet for story time. During one story I persisted in whispering to a friend several seats away, putting my hand over my mouth to prevent Mrs Munden seeing or hearing. After one warning I was sent to stand in the corner in disgrace. To make matters worse, Mother was out for a walk when I was returning home from school and met me on the Leys, a thing that she rarely did. On seeing her, a girl I often called a 'tell-tale tit' greeted her with: 'Mrs Page, Robin had to go and stand up in the corner this afternoon for being naughty,' and I was in disgrace at home as well.

My desk mate was also a tell-tale tit, but if any of the boys ever teased her, called her names, or joined me in pulling her hair, her mother would wait outside the gate for us; an obese woman with ruddy cheeks and a short tongue. If we noticed her we would loiter in the playground until she was busily engaged in gossiping to one of the other mothers, and then we would try to sneak past her unobserved.

Although life in the Little Room was generally happy, the day most eagerly awaited by all the infants was the one on which they started in the Big Room, for then they ceased to be considered as babies and became juniors. That day was even more important for me as I could then start riding to school on the blue bicycle that had become too small for both John and Mary. I did not ride it all the way, for the bicycle shed in the playground was to be avoided because of punctures and disappearing valve rubbers, and so I left it with Auntie Ruby, the unofficial aunt who had looked after us during Mother's confinement, who lived in a small house in the High Street, next to the shop opposite the chapel.

On entering the bottom class of the Big Room, I, like the other four who went with me, quickly regretted the move, which put us in a large plain room, seated at double desks, in serried ranks all facing the front and a long way from the Tortoise stove glowing close to Miss Whitmell's desk; the whole room seemed cold and formal. To make matters worse, the Big Room also housed Miss Whitmell's temper which, when in full flow, would cause her to shout, stalk up and down, shake those who were inattentive, and deal stinging blows around the ears to those who persistently gave the wrong answers.

One day she got so angry with Brian, a friend a year older than me, that she dragged him out of his desk, and holding him by the scruff of the neck, marched him to her desk, striking him firmly in the seat of his pants with her knee at every step forward. Her anger was likely to fall on anyone at any time; it fell upon John once when he stood between the stove and her desk as she marked his sums, which were nearly all wrong. 'You had better pull your socks up John Page,' she admonished severely. John, fearful and obedient, took her warning as a command, bent down and felt for his socks which he found were already pulled up; Miss Whitmell seized him, bent him over the desk and punished him with the flat of her hand for insolence.

When her patience was really tried to the limit she turned, as a last resort, to the cane, which she used very rarely. The last time she threatened to use this deterrent, apart from during P.T. when she often stung miscreants with jumping canes, the whole room was shocked into silence by an astonishing act of defiance. Two of the older girls were promised the cane for continued disobedience, but just as the punishment was to be administered in front of the whole class, Miss Whitmell remembered an urgent visit she had to make to the school house. While she was briefly away the girls quickly and silently broke the cane into a number of small pieces and dropped them behind a large cupboard. Despite Miss Whitmell's fulminations, nobody would admit to the cane's whereabouts or its fate, and the girls escaped any serious acts of retribution.

Surprisingly, one morning even Miss Whitmell realised that her temper had gone too far, and saw that instead of making the whole class work more diligently, it was making her the centre of attraction, and whenever her attention was elsewhere in the room, glances and smiles were being exchanged by those who were not the subject of her fury. As the morning progressed, so her anger built up, and a succession of unfortunates with wrong sums or bad grammar received harsh words and a fine spray of saliva in their faces. By the time Christopher was at her desk with all his arithmetic wrong, she could contain herself no longer; she banged her fist down on his exercise book in exasperation, with such venom that her bottle of red marking ink shot into the air and fell to the floor. 'Now look what you've made me do,' she shouted, and sent him back to his desk, howling and with throbbing ears. On clearing up the mess she noticed a cupboard door open: 'And who's left that open?' she demanded irritably, striding up to it and slamming it violently. There was a crash, the door split down the middle, the two halves separated and were left hanging precariously on the lowest hinge. This was the last straw, she returned to her desk, wheeled round to bark out an order, but instead of words, her top set of teeth flew out of her mouth and clattered to the floor. Hands went up to faces to conceal sniggers. Miss Whitmell picked up her dentures and hurriedly left the room to go home. After a break of several minutes, in which cautious demonstrations of temper and teeth flying out were given, she returned, her temper gone, ready to start her day again.

My first serious reprimand came after only a few days of Big Room status when she gave us new juniors a spelling test to find out how much we knew, and among the words she asked us to spell was 'Cambridgeshire'. Fortunately I remembered that this long and difficult word was printed on the cover of our exercise books, and putting my arm around my work, pretending to prevent my neighbours from copying, I surreptitiously turned over the cover, and wrote the word down. When it came to the answers Miss Whitmell asked me to spell out what I had written. Pleased with knowing this lengthy word, and sure that I was the only one with the right answer I confidently spelt out what I had written: 'C-a-m-b-r-i-g-s-h-i-r-e.'

'What,' she erupted, 'you haven't even copied it correctly you hopeless boy,' and after a shaking, during which my head felt as if it would drop off at any moment, she warned: 'And don't you ever let me catch you cheating again.'

A few days later I was in trouble once more, this time with my arithmetic. Miss Whitmell's face kept looming close to mine, grimacing with fermenting rage: 'Well,' she shouted, 'what's the answer – No, it's not, add it up again… Go on faster… What is it? Of course it's not… Come in early after your milk and do them again until they are right.'

At playtime I was moodily sucking my third of a pint of milk through a straw, standing in the porch, amid the noise and clatter of milk being taken out of the crates when a bottle suddenly shattered at my feet. Miss Whitmell charged onto the scene and on the circumstantial evidence that met her eyes assumed that I was the culprit: 'You again,' she growled through grinding teeth as she shook me by the shoulders, 'finish off your milk this instant and get on with your sums.'

This was too much. I put the bottle down and fled, rushing out of the porch, over the playground and across School Lane. There I stopped briefly to look back, the other children were all staring, amazed, and Miss Whitmell was crossing the playground waving her arms and shouting: 'Come back here.' I ran down Church Lane as fast as my legs would carry me, with fear completely conquering asthma, crossed the High Street, entered Auntie Ruby's shed, clambered onto my bike and pedalled frantically home.

Mother was most surprised to see me at such a time: 'What on earth are you doing, dear?' she asked with concern.

'Miss Whitmell got on to me for spilling milk that I didn't.' I bleated, full of self-pity.

Mother was quite unprepared for such a situation. 'Well you know you shouldn't have come home don't you? You either go straight back, or spend the day in bed.' To be sent to bed was usually considered to be a punishment, but on this day I saw it as a happy release. I rapidly disappeared upstairs and leapt into bed before Mother changed her mind. This put her in something of a dilemma; she had always taught us to keep our word, and as a result she could see no other alternative than to keep hers. At dinner she discussed the situation with Father, and managed to coax me down and onto my bike. She accompanied me across the main road and onto the Leys path, but with both brakes firmly on, I refused to go any further. That evening Mother went to see Miss Whitmell who agreed to forget the whole incident. The next day I returned slowly to school, bearing a peace offering, a bunch of grapes cut from the greenhouse.

Away from the frustrations of teaching reading, writing and arithmetic, Miss Whitmell seemed to be transformed into a different person, bringing pygmies and Eskimos into the classroom in vivid words and pictures, and describing the kings, queens, and battles of history, making them live. During P.T. she would tuck her skirt into her knickers to demonstrate how to skip, jump and climb ropes, and this change in her disposition, with its comparative freedom, came as a welcome relief. There was 'music and movement', when we all ran into the institute to follow instructions given by a lady's voice gushing from the wireless set, making ourselves into various shapes, trees,

monsters, and fairies, running round the large hall to the music and collapsing on to the floor, taking care to avoid splinters. In the afternoons there was painting, with the smell of powdered paints, the clatter of paint tins being washed up, and children mutually admiring each other's pictures. If brushes and water were knocked over, Miss Whitmell's temper would briefly reassert itself, but generally all was well. Mrs Munden helped with clay modelling, teaching us to pummel and knead the cold wet clay and mould it into the shapes of animals, vases, or anything that took our fancy. She tried to move me away from Ian one day, as we kept talking, but with my legs wrapped around the desk's legs, and my hands clasping the lid, both she and Miss Whitmell failed to dislodge me. Eventually they gave up, took the clay away and moved Ian, leaving me sulking, with nothing to do. On another occasion Martin, who was good at all artistic work, made a model of Joseph, the father of Jesus, and both teachers thought it to be outstanding for one so young. While they were out of the room I accidentally knocked if off a table as I was going past, and again Miss Whitmell broke the peace, but generally these lessons were enjoyable and ones to look forward to. The arrival of the annual puppet show was also eagerly awaited, for each year Mrs Munden dramatised a well known children's story which we performed with our puppets. We each made our own puppets with painted papier-mâché heads on a clay base, and jointed wooden bodies worked by strings. Amid excitement from us, and admiration from an audience of parents, Snow White, Dick Whittington, and Aladdin all came to miniature, jerking life.

During the more formal lessons, there were nearly always children willing to test Miss Whitmell's mood and generosity, by putting up hands and wearing pained expressions, wanting to catch her eye to ask: 'Please Miss, can I be excused,' in the hope that they could gain a few minutes respite and stroll to the toilets. The boys' toilets were at the back of the school, a small slated white-washed hut divided into three by walls not quite reaching the roof; inside there were two bucket lavatories with wooden seats, and a urinal, an odorous open gutter, that during times of boredom or persecution became a brief refuge. At playtimes, when nature called, it became almost a communal gathering place, and often when crowded, someone would see how far he could relieve himself up the wall. This was seen by many as a challenge, and we would all begin to exercise bladder and winky to see who could pee the highest; on good days some would manage to hit the ceiling, or send fountains of urine up and over the wall and onto the lavatory next door, leaving everywhere steaming, dripping and smelling even worse.

The girls' toilets were next to the school house, and due to their position, and the actual anatomy of little girls they were used correctly, although not always without incident. One new girl, not used to the high wooden seat, got into difficulties after she had received permission from Miss Whitmell to be excused. She hoisted herself onto the seat, but as her feet left the ground, so her bottom descended into the hole, forcing her knees up to her chest. She was found twenty minutes later, whimpering and stuck fast.

It was a disappointment to us boys, Brian, Ian, Chris, Dick, Dicky, another Robin, as well as to the older boys, that there were never enough of us to play football or cricket. Instead we had to play netball and shinty, a form of hockey with few rules and a rough stick that could be wielded in whatever way possible as long as an attempt was made to hit the ball. We liked these games, but preferred more manly sports which we had to leave until evenings or week-ends when we would play on our lawn or 'go up the recreation ground', which ran parallel to the Leys, and was separated from it by a large hawthorn and bramble hedge. It was on the rec that the village football team performed, including Father at full back in his long shorts and large boots, and a goalkeeper who, before each game started, would hang on the crossbar and leap spectacularly to make imaginary saves, but as soon as the whistle went he spent his time falling over, dropping the ball, and as it became wetter and heavier, retrieving it at regular intervals from the back of the net; sadly his ability to hang from the bar counted for nothing. Jack Hawkes, a local farmer, was one of the stars, tall and fast, with short shorts and long white legs; every time he got the ball we would shout; 'Come on Telegraph Pole,' or alternatively, 'Come on Daddy Long Legs,' and then fall about with laughter at our wit.

But it was cricket that became my main passion; there was no team in the village as it had disbanded several years earlier, only a rough pitch on the rec with wickets cut from the hedges and a hard ball that either created fast reflexes or sore shins. One of the highlights of each summer was a visit to Fenners (the cricket ground of Cambridge University) with Mother and Father to see cricket played in its ideal setting; a smooth green sward, a background of flowering horse chestnuts, and cricketers in white flannels, creating an atmosphere of tradition and tranquillity. When the Australians toured, Miss Whitmell reluctantly gave me permission to leave school half way through the morning to go with an old retired minister who lived near the farm, to see the second day of the match against the university. My bike had a puncture and I ran the full length of the Leys, for the first time without a wheeze to catch the bus, and spent the rest of the day watching Peter May, David Shepherd, and other less accomplished undergraduates, trying to score runs against the ferocious bowling of Lindwall and Miller.

Whatever class we were doing, P.T., or English, shinty or arithmetic, we always welcomed playtime, to finish off old games, to start new ones or, at dinner time, to wait for the dinner van in the hope of getting some 'turf' cigarette cards from the driver. The girls played hopscotch and skipping, the boys raced their Dinky toy cars or played football with a balding tennis ball on the square at the back of the school building. When the sun went down in winter, leaving open skies, stars, and the promise of frost, the older boys tipped buckets of water over it to freeze and give us slides as clear and as treacherous as glass. After school, our winter sports moved down to the pond where long slides would stretch from one side to the other. It was on the pond as a thaw was setting in that an accident befell me for, as we were defying the ominous cracks and groans with acts of foolish bravado, the ice suddenly splintered around me and I fell into the numbing water up to my waist. When I arrived home wet and wheezing, Mother made me sit with my feet in a bowl of hot water until I ceased to shiver.

Four large old elm trees with gnarled trunks stood in the playground, one at the front, with a hook screwed into a branch from which a rope was suspended for P.T., and the other three were in a row along one side. They were ideal for chasing games like 'tig' and variations of it. Kiss chase, which was played only if Miss Whitmell and Mrs Munden were safely out of sight, when kisses were administered behind one of the trees, and 'witty' in which those caught joined hands until a great chain of children swept the playground in pursuit of those still free, with screams and laughter filling the air. 'Big A, little a, bouncing b,

cat's in the cupboard and can't see me,' was another favourite pastime, when someone posed as the cat trying to spot others creeping up behind, as was 'Sheep, sheep, come home', involving a shepherd and his flock separated by the width of the playground, which contained a number of wolves.

'Sheep, sheep, come home,' the shepherd would call.

'We can't.'

'Why not?'

'The wolf.'

'The wolf has gone to Devonshire and won't be back for eleven years; sheep, sheep, come home.' With that, the flock had to dash to their shepherd, while the wolves appeared from behind the girls' lavatories to try and add to their number.

Outside the classroom and the playground, Miss Whitmell was keenly aware of the beauty around us, and her nature walks, when we would leave the blackboard and desks far behind were always eagerly anticipated. In twos we would walk along School Lane, past the vicarage, where the wall suddenly stopped and amid an overgrown part of the garden a black shallow pool of stagnant water, where it was said a servant girl had drowned herself many years before, could be seen. It looked foul and ominous, but in the autumn our attention was drawn elsewhere by the large beech trees nearby that sprinkled the lane with nuts which we would collect and hoard in our pockets to chew on our journey.

The path took us past the planton and over the road to the pond, where we would briefly stop to kneel on the bank, looking through our reflections and deep into the water, searching with alert eyes for newts, leeches, and water boatmen. On we would go past a smaller pond, velvet black, with matching moorhens scurrying from it, jerking their white tails nervously. Past an ever-changing bank of roadside flowers, cowslips, buttercups, vetches, finger and thumbs, cornflowers, chicory and poppies. Past the 'Five Houses', and the roadman with his sleeves rolled up, his waistcoat undone, leaning on his broom watching us pass, and

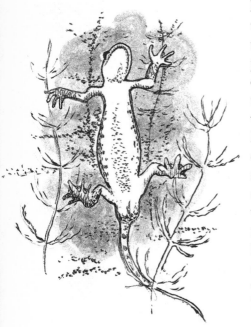

then we would leave the path and turn to cart tracks and bridle paths, passing through stack yards and over fields to the rifle range (a military range – occasionally used at week-ends). As we walked, we heard larks high in the sky, balanced on dizzy spirals of song, saw rooks on ragged wings wheeling nonchalantly on thermals of scorched air, and we would sing 'a little bit of bread and no cheese', mimicking the yellow hammers. If we were lucky, we caught glimpses of stoats or weasels, with dark piercing eyes, and sleek bodies, and then after a rest we would slowly return, picking wild flowers, with dust steadily drifting into our sandals and settling between our toes.

The village flower show was always held towards the end of July, in a small grass meadow lined with giant horse chestnuts next to the pond. As the great day approached, we all collected armfuls of flowers and grasses to stuff into jam jars in an effort to win a small prize, believing firmly in quantity rather than quality. We were all expected to enter, as we were for the clay modelling and painting competitions, and the few weeks before the show we worked busily on our entries, with Mrs Munden and Miss Whitmell watching but rarely helping. By the day of the show, a large marquee was erected in the field, and inside our entries were displayed, together with lesser fare, plates of ripe, hairy gooseberries, collections of enormous runner beans, vegetables and fruit of all shapes and sizes, flowers, cakes and pots of jam. All the village seemed to be there, and as soon as the show had been officially opened by a local dignitary who addressed the gathering from a trailer, everyone circulated, talking, moving on, talking again, in one endless round. There were stalls selling jumble and home-made produce, a rifle range, a contraption at which balls were thrown to tip a lady out of bed, as well as our old grey donkey who was ridden by children for 1d a time.

Those children who had won prizes eagerly searched for their parents and friends, while the successful gardeners with winning carrots or cabbages and the ladies with certificates of merit for their gingerbread, were just as pleased, but suppressed their joy behind masks of false modesty. The afternoon finished with children's sports; sprints, egg and spoon, wheelbarrow, sack and three-legged races, involving both children and parents. This routine was only broken once, in 1953, when a special sports day was held on the recreation ground to celebrate the Coronation of the new Queen Elizabeth; then there were even more races than usual, and medals to be won, each one bearing the Queen's head. Some of the bigger boys won handfuls of medals, but I managed to win only one, for finishing third in a sack race. I pinned it to my shirt, wearing it as proudly as if it had been the Victoria Cross, and ran home to show it to Mother. John entered all the races he could, anxious to win a medal too, but he always finished just out of the first three, losing his egg or falling over his sack.

As the afternoon wore on he became progressively more quiet, until he could contain his disappointment no longer; he moved away from the happy crowd to cry.

Apart from art at the flower show, another school activity was demonstrated in public each year, when a selection of the best dancers were asked to perform country dancing on the vicarage lawn at the church fete. That was a much more reserved village occasion, when polite conversation, large flowered hats, the clatter of dainty tea cups, and bowling for a pig, all mingled uneasily. Mr Howes taught us country dancing, sometimes coming to the school, while in summer, when it was fine, we all trooped up to his large garden at Five Houses, where we danced to the accompaniment of a gramophone that had to be vigorously wound up after every dance. He was an unusual man, tall, erect, with penetrating grey eyes and a quiet manner that remained unruffled however chaotic the dances became and regardless of the number of times we forgot simple movements. His father had been an artist and Mr Howes retained an air of detached refinement, sustained by a diet of literature and fine arts. In 1914 he had joined the Artists' Rifles, in which he was made an officer, on his discharge he worked in a bank, where he became a manager, and by the time he came to teach us dancing he was leading a comfortable and cultured retirement. The five houses, which were really bungalows, were built by him in memory of his five sisters, and it was on a lawn at the back that we danced, usually in the sun, our lungs full of air sweet with the scent of roses, honeysuckle and wallflowers. As summer proceeded, we were rewarded at the end of each dancing afternoon with apples picked from an old orchard beyond the lawn.

Strangely, despite being friendly, Mr Howes always remained slightly aloof, and although he was regularly seen around the village, walking, sitting on a marble seat near his house, or riding his bicycle, he never seemed to be a real part of it. Because of this, and his habit of disappearing to Tangiers for a month in winter, rumours spread about him. Some said he was an atheist, others considered him to be a communist involved in an international conspiracy and some hinted at other things, stemming from the fact that he was unmarried. But the story which I found most interesting and which I found most difficult to believe suggested that he went to bed wearing a long white nightshirt together with matching knitted hat.

In addition to all the normal activities of school, Miss Whitmell also managed the occasional surprise. With no prior warning she suddenly announced one afternoon an unprecedented prizegiving, and placed a large pile of books on her desk. Nearly everyone was presented with a book, and I received one entitled *Fifteen Rabbits* for 'a good term's work and good handwriting': the only time that my hand-writing was ever commended or that I received a reward for academic work. It was a story about rabbits, written by the author of *Bambi* and published according to the 'war economy standard'. I read it avidly, taking it to bed with me and when one of the rabbits came to a violent end I buried my head in my pillow and sobbed bitterly. Just as it was the first prizegiving we had ever known, so it was the last, but it was a day when the shoutings and shakings seemed worthwhile, and Miss Whitmell's face radiated pleasure.

Again, several years before rationing ended – rationing started during the Second World War and was not lifted until 3 July, 1954 with the decontrol of meat and bacon – she suddenly placed a large wooden box emblazoned with red crosses on her desk. Then, as we all waited expectantly she emptied out its contents; a number of smaller packages, just enough for each of us to have one. They were American Red Cross parcels which we all opened enthusiastically. I unwrapped mine to find a bag of sugar, a jar of jam, and tin of beef in gravy that, at my insistence, Mother heated up and served the next day; but the gift that I liked best was a black yo-yo, which started a craze lasting several weeks.

These parcels were not the only reminders of scarcity and the fact that the war was not long over. Some children had to start each day with a spoonful of malt and cod liver oil, fed to them by Miss Whitmell from extra large jars. At home, in the broom cupboard, Father's tin helmet, gas mask, and warden's greatcoat still hung from the door, as they had since the time he had worn them for night observation from the top of the church tower. In the toy cupboard were three smaller gas masks, green, and decorated with pictures of Mickey Mouse, and Mother continued to salt beans and preserve eggs in waterglass as she had during hostilities. Military convoys also went past regularly and then it became too dangerous to ride our bikes on the road or to race them round the triangle of grass outside the farm where a small country road joined the main road, which was not much bigger. One convoy lasted for three whole days and nights, with a continuous stream of armoured cars, troop carriers and field guns heading, so it was said, for manoeuvres on Salisbury Plain. That particular armour-plated procession was English, but we preferred American convoys, and whenever we heard the rumble of heavy lorries and saw painted stars, we rushed across the road to join Christopher and his brother to wave, and to shout 'Any gum chum?' In response, soldiers with brush cuts, or black smiling faces would throw us bubble gum or chocolate, which we scrummaged for in the grass, but always shared.

The school outing, when Miss Whitmell and a coach load of children and mothers visited London, was more of an annual surprise; the city, we were told, was the capital of Britain and the Empire, in which the King lived, and where there were marvels unknown

elsewhere; the zoo, guardsmen wearing bearskins, Buckingham Palace, Kew Gardens, Hampton Court, and in 1951, the Festival of Britain. There we saw all manner of famous things and famous people; a procession of national figures including two old bald men, our leaders, Churchill and Attlee, together with various royal personages, all attending the laying of the foundation stone for the Royal Festival Hall. Later in the day we saw Bluebird, fresh from a new land speed record and wonders of the past, as well as of the future, and a specially constructed fountain, like a monument of pivoting coal buckets, that were forever filling with water, tipping over to empty, then righting themselves to refill, making a continuous cascade of splashing water.

As time went by, progress was made quite literally up the Big Room, from one end to the other, passing the stove half way along. The older boys left, including John; Rachael started, and by the time I arrived in the top class things seemed to be different. Physically, the old Tortoise fire had gone, to be replaced by a new coke stove surrounded by an even larger semicircular wire guard. Old Flo the caretaker still lit it each day during cold weather, but even her job had altered and become easier. Due to the proximity of the churchyard, there had been no water fit to drink when I started in the Little Room, and Flo had carried a bucket of pure water to school every morning taken from the pump outside her house in the High Street. Now chlorinated water was available from the mains.

Miss Whitmell seemed to have changed too, and as she prepared us for the eleven plus examination, we found her much less intimidating. She still lost her temper from time to time, but we learned to ignore it. Once during my final year, while she was in her house after giving us instructions to work quietly, I gave the class a demonstration of whooping, as there was a whooping cough epidemic raging. The whoops were so healthy that they reverberated around not only the school, but also the school house, bringing Miss Whitmell storming back over the playground and into the classroom. She shouted and threatened, but by then I had mastered the art, like most of the top class, of looking penitent while being secretly amused.

Even her physical punishments seemed less of a threat, for as we grew bigger, so she seemed to get smaller. Every Monday morning we listened to *Singing Together*, when we joined in song with the radio singers. Half way through the last programme that I would ever listen to, Miss Whitmell ordered me to leave the room for talking instead of singing; I wanted to stay and sat firm. She took hold of one of my arms and, on this occasion, managed to haul me from my desk and pull me towards the door. I struggled to hold my ground, but with my shoes slipping on the polished floor she was winning, until the fireguard was reached, when I firmly gripped it with my free hand. For several seconds we both stood tugging, until suddenly the guard jumped from its sockets, allowing Miss Whitmell to lead me and the fireguard out of the room in linked single file. Once in the porch she left me and retreated back inside, taking the guard with her; she considered that she had won, but I thought it had been an honourable draw.

Michael, a quiet, tall, new boy got off much less lightly, for he was quite unused to teachers like Miss Whitmell. She was convinced that he could learn, he was equally convinced that he could not and as a result, every time his sums were wrong Miss Whitmell tried to drum the correct information into him, stopping only when his crying made it impossible to continue. To make matters worse, because of his unusual height, and his mild Yorkshire accent, we ostracised him and, as everybody else was intimidated by his size, I challenged him to a fight after school on the Leys. With Dicky, Ian and Chris around me I was confident of victory, and decided that my best tactics would be to trip him up, and then sit on him until he gave in.

Throwing our bikes down on the grass the battle began: I seized him round the waist as planned and pushed him backwards over my foot. Then to complete the move, as he fell I tried to jump on him to hold him down. Unfortunately I had not anticipated much resistance and as I fell down onto him, his fist came up, hitting me in the mouth. Pain shot through my lower jaw, and as I scrambled to my feet, I cupped my hands, spitting blood and bits of teeth into them. A lady nearby who had seen the fight in progress brought me a glass of water and told Michael that he was a bully, and should pick on someone his own size. He was frightened and hurried home; crestfallen, I was taken to the dentist and even now the gap remains.

When the eleven plus results were finally announced we had

104

nearly all passed to go to grammar schools of various sorts, and we were allowed home to tell our parents. Miss Whitmell was openly pleased, not because her remarkable record of passes had been maintained, but because she had 'got us on'. Nearly every year over half of those who sat the exam passed, causing parents from other villages and even Cambridge itself to try and get their children admitted to the school. She rarely accepted them, for she had no more room and, in any case, she saw herself primarily as the village schoolmistress, sent to serve the parish, not as an educator in search of a reputation.

She was not only interested in those who passed exams, and followed careers of all her old pupils, whether they became doctors or dustmen. A result of her dedication was that ordinary village children from ordinary village homes were given the opportunity to go to universities and colleges after which they obtained jobs thought to be virtually unobtainable just a generation before; one went as a student to the Cambridge college where his father was a gardener, others became teachers, a doctor, a chartered quantity surveyor, an air hostess, a laboratory technician, and even Michael, after failing the eleven plus went to university and got a degree. But whatever her old pupils did, and wherever they went, most remembered Miss Whitmell with real affection; they remembered their tables, and how to spell 'Cambridgeshire' as well.

CHAPTER 6

The Brook

———

The brook formed the southern boundary of the parish, gently cutting into clay as it flowed between wooded banks and wandered through water meadows on its way to join the River Cam, just above a sluice and tree-lined pool, where Rupert Brook and Lord Byron had once sought solitude. Its meanders spread in a series of time smoothed curves, winding across a broad flood plain which gradually rose on either side to form the slightest of green grass valleys. Close by the water's edge, rushes and sedges grew, giving way on drier ground to bushes, shrubs and tall mature willows, some fractured by long forgotten autumnal gales, their limbs torn and bent over into water, forming the foundations of large natural dams. The neighbouring fields were hedged by ancient elms and thorns and had been grazed by sheep and cattle for as far back as local memory could recall; now Father's cows and bullocks did likewise, pulling at the luxuriant pastures and swishing their tails to keep off flies.

In summer, the brook itself was a mixture of gravel shallows and deep murky pools, of water lilies, yellow irises, and reed mace; while

in winter it was grey, cold and silent, reflecting only the season of the year. In a bramble thicket on one of its banks I saw my first fox, briefly frozen in memory before disappearing into the long grass behind, and one summer an elderly fisherman watched a family of otters at play among the submerged roots of an old hawthorn tree. Below the surface of the water, fish grew fat and plentiful with few anglers to concern them, and above, the occasional kingfisher flew in a straight brittle line of incandescent turquoise, and a solitary heron regularly landed on slow arched wings, to stand grey and still, its yellow eyes full of the burden of loneliness, peering into the water, its stilt-like legs motionless and its dagger bill pointing downwards, ready.

Father's fields bordered the northern bank of the brook and followed it from Lord's Bridge, running eastwards up to another road bridge and beyond for a total of one and a half miles or more. Our domain also started at Lord's Bridge, where the water was deep, the bed was straight, a cramped spinney of sallow in marsh and buttercups stood on one side and warblers nested in the reeds. This point of the brook had been straightened many years before to allow the bridge to be constructed; previously, local legend told, there had been only a ford, where, when the brook was in full spate, a traveller had been swept away and drowned, which suggested to a benevolent Lord that he should build a bridge. Part of an old meander, now isolated, remained in Father's field as a pond, together with a number of shallow holes and hollows where seams of gravel had been dug out until well after the First World War. Those wanting material for buildings or roadways had arrived with horses and carts to dig out their requirements, but better quality sand and gravel obtained mechanically had replaced its need, and grass had covered all its cliffs and undulations. We used it as an occasional dirt track for our bikes and hundreds of rabbits had made it into home, forming a large rabbit warren, riddled with holes.

Tit Brook, narrow and straight, formed the northern perimeter of the warren, bubbling clear and shallow over sand, shingle and three small man-made dams. It flowed through steep banks, which flattened where an old bridge, now collapsed, had once stood, lining the bed with rubble and allowing the cattle to stand, unsinking, to drink.

It flowed into the main brook almost opposite the mouth of another cool, clear stream that had its source three miles away, deep in chalk. The two streams between them had transported tons of sand and shingle to drop into the brook, building a substantial barrage which held the water upstream, deep and dark beneath a canopy of willow. The water usually ran swiftly with no depth over the obstruction, rattling stones as if exhilarated by movement and release, but in times of drought the brook stood almost still, apart from the streams, which, blocked by their own silt, trickled into the deep, giving it the appearance of flowing slightly backwards.

Beyond the entrance of Tit Brook was an area of boggy, stagnant mud, in which grew dense clusters of blackthorn where hedge sparrows nested unperturbed among the poisoned points of wood, and gnats flew in endless dizziness. Past this gloom the banks freshened, with occasional trees, willow, sallow, and hawthorn, and the brook's shape and flow changed to suit every mood; short swift races, deep swirling eddies, the soothing tinkle of water washing over pebbles, or falling over broken branches, and stillness, where water lilies floated on the surface with their roots deep and static below. Next, a stretch of shallows where the knotted roots of reed mace supported a legion of upturned pokers every year, and halfway between the two bridges, where the meadow was divided by a hedge, a grassy bank met the water, making it possible to sit and dangle our naked legs to find fresh water mussels with our feet and dream of bringing to the surface a large shell, empty except for a pearl. Opposite, among a small grove of large elms was an even more populous rabbit warren, with rabbits young and old watching warily, nibbling daintily with white cotton tails ready to bob in warning. Rabbits were in evidence everywhere, keeping that field grazed like a lawn and spilling over the brook, along the hedges of Father's meadows and further on still, to eat the tender shoots of barley and wheat.

Just past the second bridge was the dace pool, where insects were sucked beneath the surface in sudden swirls and flashes of turning silver darted beneath the ripples. As the pool tapered, the water ran fast over rubble, passing an old public wash pit, into which small rivulets still seeped. Shepherds had at one time washed their sheep there and surrounding it, briefly interrupting Father's meadows, was a small field known as 'the jungle'; an overgrown area of wildness and damp, which was never used. Then came another small field belonging to Father with a hedge marking its final boundary; but the brook flowed on, with grass meadows and hedges following its bends for as far as the eye could see.

From our Big Room days until well on into our teens, the brook meadows became our regular haunt. Every Sunday, either alone, with John or Chris, or occasionally with Mother and Father, I walked along the bank, hot in the sun or with raw winds lashing rain into my face, stopping hopefully at every unexpected splash, sudden movement of rush, or acrid whiff of fox, and each week the whole character of the area seemed to change, sometimes subtly, at other times more obviously. During holidays it became one large play-ground, where pursuits and mock battles occurred, dams and bridges were constructed and fishing expeditions took place. Each season brought something different to occupy us and each year the seasons varied.

Spring started in March 'down the brook', after snowdrops in the garden, and before the last straggling groups of fieldfares had flown in their gently wave-like flight to far-off forests in Scandinavia. It was marked by the arrival of frogs at Lord's Bridge, for as the sun shone fractionally brighter, an indefinable stirring could be detected in the air, and the frogs were the first to feel it and wake from hibernation. We rarely actually saw them, but in the pond and puddles of the gravel workings, spawn appeared in great gelatinous masses, like pools of floating sago. Only once did Chris and myself witness the adult frogs in the act of spawning, when on a cold cloudy day we approached the pond from a small clump of willow and thorn, and through the bare branches we saw dozens of blunt brown heads and eyes protruding from beneath the surface. The wind and water were icy, and the clouds looked as if they bore the last of winter's snow, but the frogs, lying still, were creating new life and heralding a new season.

Squashed frogs were always to be seen on the road near the bridge at this time and soon the enclosed pools of water were teeming with tadpoles. Nearly every year we collected some to take home, housing them in a bowl placed in the bath, and there we watched them gradually grow into exact miniature replicas of their parents. Each year, too, we went with buckets to Lord's Bridge, for as the wind grew warmer and drier, so the water level dropped, turning puddles into seething black masses of tadpoles and sludge, which we scooped up and transported to the pond. The success of our mission could be seen later, after a heavy shower of rain, or while dew still dampened the grass, for tiny frogs would leap to avoid descending feet, or dive into the brook, disappearing beneath a stream of silver bubbles into the deep.

The march of spring advanced with a steady build up of the dawn chorus, moles digging up mounds of clean earth and the grass freshening. Cowslips appeared in the meadows, violets in the hedgerows, and buds grew to burst into verdant foliage. Rooks and blackbirds were among the first to start incubating new eggs, as were mallards in the trunk-held crevices of old willows, cock pheasants fought, and hares chased in their mating madness.

Sedge and reed began to grow, willow warblers sent their bubbling song cascading from the tree tops, and after the white 'may' of thorn had come and gone, sometimes with its brief spell of 'blackthorn winter', marsh marigolds ornamented the banks and yellow iris held their flags to the breeze. Moorhens built raft-like nests in midstream, dapper male reedbuntings in hirsute smartness appeared to sport well groomed black beards and bibs, and green woodpeckers, each with a crimson crown, sent out their ringing laughter as they flew in lazy undulations from tree to tree.

Pike basked close to the surface of the deep water, near Tit Brook, in willow pattern patches of dancing sunlight; roach, dace, and shoals

110

of 'tiddlers', sticklebacks and minnows swam in the shallows, eating and hiding in the rich green beds of spreading starwort. The flowering cup-curved petals of watercrowfoot bedecked the surface of the pond which, surrounded by rustling beds of wind-bent reeds, seemed to generate heat. Mayflies and mosquitoes danced, and the mud-brown nymphs of damsel and dragon flies hauled themselves into the air, to rest on the stems of sedges and wait for solar reincarnation. As the sun charged them with energy, their wings uncurled, iridescent and quivering, and their bodies absorbing heat, glowed red, green, or blue, as they flickered into flight, hovering and darting, reflecting the colours of the rainbow.

Grass snakes were sometimes to be seen hunting among the beds of watercress in Tit Brook, dog roses gave splashes of soft, fragrant pink to the hedgerows, the meadows grew yellow with buttercups, and we added wisps of white to the air by blowing dandelion clocks. In the Jungle, elms, saplings and ancient trees cast patches of cooling shade, cow parsley, hemlock, hogweed, and wild angelica made a carpet of swaying white, held aloft on fragile stems, and patches of white dead nettle, bindweed, mallow, and clover, offered up sweeter scents to the breath of wind. Jackdaws fed their noisy young, flycatchers darted here and there from one perch to another in pursuit of food, sparrows clumsily chased butterflies and everywhere was the hum of insects in airborne industry. Large ant hills gave vantage points from which to gaze after bumble bees as they droned by, or from where the undergrowth could be simply scanned; concealed in a clump of coarse grass near one ant-citadel I found a blind, naked, newly born animal, but not knowing what it was I covered it up again and left it for its mother who must have been close by.

Each evening as the light began to fade, the pungent tang of mud and sedge replaced the gentle fragrance of the day and mist formed in patches of steam-white as the air cooled over the brook. Barn owls the same colour as the mist floated onto fence posts, their dark unblinking eyes waking to yet another day of night and then, on silent wings they quartered the meadows in search of voles, mice and young rabbits.

Summer was the most favourable time of the year for damming Tit Brook and with rubble and mud we would block its flow completely to capture stranded sticklebacks in jam jars. Angry males with blood-red breasts were particularly prized, as were bullheads; ugly scaled fish with large heads and flapping fins, like miniature prehistoric monsters. Bullheads were also caught in a small pool where the water fell over one of the dams, when hands suddenly clasped at fins beneath a stone or brick and hoisted out one of the slimy creatures to drop into a jar. I disliked the feel of their horny gums and squirming bodies and stuck to hunting sticklebacks.

Fishing in a more orthodox way, with a variety of home-made and second-hand rods, with thick lines and large hooks, was also popular. Worms, cheese, and bread, were all dangled at varying depths and roach and a variety of tiddlers were often caught. Evenings among the gnats at the dace pool were similarly successful, with water and bank voles busily gnawing at rushes to watch, when the fish were not biting, and a meal of fried dace to taste when they were.

We nearly all had visions of hooking really huge fish that we knew to be there. The elderly fisherman had caught plenty always putting them back, and he told of large pike trying to chew their way into his keep net. There were, in addition, said to be a large bream and even tench, which could be caught with a combination of skill and patience. Lord's Bridge was thought by us to shelter the largest fish of all, for it was there that we caught the best roach, and we had seen a giant pike with vicious jaws basking near by, looking almost as deep as it was long. Michael told us that he would provide further evidence of large fish, when he produced a bag of cloud bait which, he insisted, would attract them by the shoal, and to prove his point he threw handfuls of the meal into the water. We expected them to arrive quickly, anxious to give themselves up on our hooks, but none came. As we abandoned fishing for the day, Michael made the remainder of his failed bait into a sticky ball and threw it into the brook in disgust. We could just see it resting on the bottom, about the size of a fist, in five feet of water; suddenly dark jaws closed from nowhere and it disappeared.

I thought I was about to catch the elusive prize for which we had all waited, one afternoon as I sat on the bridge with my line dropped into the centre of a small clear patch of water, surrounded by a mass of floating weed; the others were fishing in various places under and beside the bridge. Again, we had had no luck until, without warning, my float began to bob as if champing jaws were eating the worm and about to seize the hook. Twice I struck and both times the hook was bare, with no worm and no fish. I carefully placed another worm on the hook and almost immediately the float resumed its bobbing and agitation. I struck again, the hook stuck fast, the rod bent, and I cried out that I had got one; what, I did not know, but presumed it to be a record-breaking perch or even pike. The others ran to join me on the bridge, it was obviously the huge fish we had anticipated. I heaved and wound, the prize was gradually being dragged reluctantly to the surface, the rod bent still further, there was considerable splashing, and a large wriggling eel noisily emerged. I was terrified, it seemed enormous. 'What do I do?' I cried out in alarm. The others stood speechless, stunned by this squirming leviathan. The problem suddenly solved itself; the rod became lighter, the eel fell back into the water and disappeared – the hook had snapped in two. The thread being used for line had a breaking strain of twenty pounds, tied to a large eel hook, the sort we nearly all used as smaller hooks were lost too readily; I was secretly delighted as well as relieved that the terrifying snake-like creature had got away.

Whenever it became very hot we longed for a swim and if we decided on one, we had to ride two miles, some of the way over a dusty bridle path, to swim in the Cam as it flowed through the near-by village of Grantchester. A stretch of gravel and quite shallow water allowed us to swim in safety and learners to manoeuvre themselves with one foot on the bottom. Christopher, it is true, did have an unexpected soaking nearer home one chilly day, when Ian and Dicky set about him in annoyance, held him to the ground and rolled him fully clothed over the bank and into the middle of Tit Brook, but we really wanted something better.

Father decided to come to our assistance and told us that he would make us a swimming place. Taking his scythe with him to the brook he cut the reeds away from the edge, and then plunged in among the yellow water lilies mid-way between Tit Brook and the bridge. We cautiously followed, our footsteps sending up clouds of black mud and the wash putting young moorhens to fright. Getting out took far longer than getting in, with our feet sinking into the ooze and leeches attaching themselves to our legs. The experiment failed and we all had to return to our respective homes for a bath.

Undeterred, Father tried again, near the otter's hawthorn tree, in water where the old man had fished. This time there were nettles and thistles to clear, but on entering the water he found gravel at the bottom. We all went in and, although retaining the smell of brook in our hair, we did not require a bath afterwards. Several summers we swam there, sometimes being joined by Mother and Grandmother, at last without her waterwings, and it was there that I learnt to dive; diving in at an angle so as not to hit the other bank.

When the days shortened and harvest was over, the feel of autumn seemed to reach the brook meadows before anywhere else. The leaves of the brambles dulled and became blotched with brown and dew was strung in droplets of watery pearl until late into the mornings, when weakening shafts of sunlight finally penetrated the mists. At weekends men and women bearing large baskets, both local and from the town, arrived to pick blackberries and before most people were up George Disbrey, who lived in the cottage next door to where I was born, and whose brothers lived in the High Street, went gathering mushrooms, which were so plentiful that he always gave some to us. Hips, haws, and the berries of woody nightshade tinged the hedges with rustiness and red, goldfinches pecked at the heads of the teasels, snipe returned to probe into the mud and as the sun dropped lower in the sky, its rays lit up dying thistles with their tufts of down, making them appear like candelabras aflame with white light.

The leaves fell, spells of prolonged rain came, the turgid pools were flushed with silt-filled water and the shallows turned into raging torrents. Several times each winter the brook overflowed its banks, spilling water over the hard grazed grass and driving those cattle still out on to higher ground, to wait patiently to be fed or driven back to the farm and a dry yard. The low valley became a river of brown swirling water rushing beneath the bridges and carrying off fences. Foam and driftwood collected on barbed wire and the naked trees stood half submerged, stark and grey. When the clouds rolled away we would make for the floods to wade in our wellington boots, trying to reach trees and small islands without getting wet feet; we nearly always reached our destination, but with our boots full of water. Excitement was caused when Christopher won a canoe in a newspaper competition, which meant that we could go anywhere, and keep our feet dry.

As the sun began to set we would start our journey home, watching as we went the water reflecting dusk in broad paths of burnished gold. The sound of restless water sang in our ears and sometimes the liquid call of passing curlews joined the whisper of wind in the branches; there seemed to be a message of freedom and eternity caught in the air.

It was during a flood that we hoped for frost, for stars, clear skies, and mornings of hoary white when even breath seemed to freeze and the tractors refused to start. The fields and garden would become as iron, and each evening after school we would hurry to the pond and brook to test the ice. After two or three nights of persistent cold we would frighten ourselves trying to be first to cross from bank to bank, ignoring the loud warning cracks and groans as we went. Then, when it was strong enough to take our jumping and falling, it was ready for skating. All types of skates emerged, old Fen Runners fixed to wood and strapped on to shoes, others that were screwed to boots; skates handed down from uncles and great-grandmothers, and even skates for figure skating with the serrated edges of the brakes filed away. The pond held first and there we would have races and competitions to see who could turn corners the fastest, all for the excitement of colliding or falling and sliding out of control over the slippery surface. Adults joined us, Father with his fast Canadian skates, Mother, Grandmother, ever game, and various others. The learners pushed chairs ahead of them for support, while most glided endlessly from one end of the pond to the other.

Some evenings, Father drove the car over the rabbit warren, dazzling scores of rabbits on the way, to shine the headlights along the brook. With cold, burning cheeks, and woollen hats, jumpers and movement giving warmth elsewhere, the clear moon above, the sound of cold steel cutting across deep frozen ice, and skaters weaving beneath stooping branches, they were the evenings that came all too infrequently.

Snow, when it arrived, often stopped the skating, having to be swept off before it fused with the ice to spoil it, but other activities followed in its wake. The fields gave secrets unnoticed before, showing up the tracks of rabbits, foxes, and the wing prints of startled pheasants. Where it drifted through the hedges we would run and dive head-first into the snowy depths and we towed an old iron stepladder to the top of the railway bridge to hurtle down the other side using it as a sledge. The birds seemed to dislike the cold, perching with ruffled feathers, and the barn owls moved ghost-like, as if carved from the frozen snow itself.

Nothing we did or saw was new, for earlier generations of children, including Mother and Father, had roamed and played in the same places and in identical ways many years before. All remained unchanged until well into the mid 1950s when myxomatosis struck the rabbits. We read of the disease's progress in the paper, but it seemed a long time reaching us and perhaps, we thought, it would miss us completely; then one day, Jim found a rabbit, helpless, with swollen discharging red eyes, blind and emaciated. Myxomatosis had arrived and it swept through the parish like plague. Soon all the rabbit warrens were deserted, except for corpses, and rabbit pie became a thing of the past. The spread of death among the rabbits was met with mixed feelings, for although they did much damage, they were a plentiful source of cheap food, the paperman would deliver them with the morning papers at 1s 2d each, and most people were sickened by their suffering and helped the slowly dying on their way with quick blows to the head.

Even so, it seemed that otherwise the brook meadows would keep the same for years to come; an area of real tranquillity, beauty and peace. Fields full of cattle quietly grazing, pike basking near the surface of the brook, wild gales cracking the willows, the sun gilding the flooded valley with rippling seams of silver, and children in harmless liberation.

CHAPTER 7

The Shoot

———

Myxomatosis seemed a hideous disease to me; an infection introduced by men completely callously, causing the rabbits to die and their bodies to rot in the fields or underground, all to no purpose. Right from my very earliest days I had always hated death, or the humiliation of life, when they had no real justification. During an early visit to Gills Hill, Cousin John had amused us in the harvest field by catching harvester spiders and pulling their legs off one by one, just to see the limbs twitch, and he would leave one – or two-legged spiders rolling helplessly on the ground. He did the same with 'daddy long legs', causing them to try and land on legless bodies or, for a change, he pulled their wings off so that they could not fly; after the initial fascination had worn off, the sport filled me with disgust.

I experienced similar feelings when, on a Sunday school outing to Whipsnade Zoo, we saw a group of children throwing empty ice cream tubs into the ostrich enclosure; with the ungainly birds trying to swallow the containers. Some succeeded and the shapes of empty cartons slowly moved down their long thin necks, while the throwers shrieked with delight and clamoured for more money from their parents to buy another lot of ice cream.

But I, too, was far from innocent, for once while pursuing mice 'up the threshing tackle field', I managed to trap a live mouse in a large steep-sided puddle. There I forced it to swim backwards and forwards; each time it reached one side I prodded it back into the water with a stick to make it swim again. Unfortunately my fascination was greater than its reserves of stamina, for gradually its frightened swimming slowed, its fur and body became weighted with water, and it stood huddled and shivering at the water's edge. Not satisfied I forced it back once more, until it finally dragged itself to the side, life left its eyes, water trickled from its mouth and sodden coat, and it died; I squeezed water from its lungs, but it would not revive and I moved away, full of guilt at the miserable death I had caused.

Later, after John had been given an air gun, we were joined by Michael on a sparrow shoot, and again we did something which made us all feel ashamed. Unfortunately, around the farm buildings we could find no sparrows, so we took the gun over to Warners Corner spinney. There we saw only blue tits, chaffinches and robins until, just as we were getting bored, a dark brown tawny owl flew from an elm and settled in the top branches of another. As soon as it perched one of us fired a pellet into the foliage above its head, making it fly off again in alarm. This, we thought was fine entertainment and we followed it through the spinney and sent a slug whistling past every time it settled. We took it in turns to fire, each one trying to shoot nearer than the last. Our sport finally stopped unexpectedly when after one shot the bird fluttered to the ground with a pellet-broken wing; this posed a problem, for if we had taken it home we would have had to explain why we had been firing at it. Instead, as it backed away, its good wing arched to frighten us, John killed it and we hurriedly buried its limp downy body in a shallow grave hastily dug at the bottom of a dry ditch.

Killing for food, or quickly disposing of pests that were obviously harmful and less attractive than rabbits, was much less deplorable however, and seemed to be a normal part of life. Every Boxing Day morning before the rabbit warren at Lord's Bridge died, Father, Jim, Charlie Lewis, Mike Sewell, Tom Murkin, Charlie's brother, and others would arrive with guns, spades and dogs to go rabbiting. In addition, Charlie Lewis took with him a wooden box that contained his prize possessions; ferrets. They were long and slender animals with sharp eyes and sharper teeth, impatient to be released into the dark holes and tunnels where, when they smelt blood, the wildness of their polecat ancestors returned. Nets were put over the bolt-holes, long cords were attached to the collars of some of the ferrets and the morning's sport was begun. The fear of death forced the first rabbits to run in blind terror into the nets, and those that followed and reached open ground faced twelve bore shot and barking dogs in excited pursuit. On occasions the ferrets would track rabbits along dead end underground passageways until all movement stopped, in a position of fearful stalemate. 'The bloody old rabbits are arsed up,' Jim would say, meaning that their heads faced a solid wall of earth and the ferret behind was unable to get at them. When this happened with a lead ferret, the distance the animal had covered underground was measured by knots tied at intervals along the line, its direction was guessed, and digging was started at the estimated place, to capture the rabbits and to retrieve the ferret. At the end of one such dig, six rabbits were pulled out unconscious and suffocating, all crushed together in fright. After a few minutes they began to revive, breathing in the fresh air; but before they had time to run off their necks were broken with fatal chops to the back of the head. When a loose ferret was used it, too, had to be dug out occasionally, with a line ferret being put down the hole to locate it. Often it would be found curled up asleep on a dead rabbit, sleeping off the effects of its meal after having killed and eaten its fill. If a ferret line broke, it was more difficult to recapture the ferret and attempts had to be made to coax it out with a dead rabbit. On almost the last such Boxing Day morning, Charlie Lewis lost one of his best ferrets, which disappeared underground and refused to come out. The inherited centuries of semi-domestication were quickly lost, the diet of bread and milk was quickly forgotten, and those living close to the warren had to shut their hens up at night.

Ferreting, along with shooting, snaring and trapping, was seen as part of the normal cycle of the hunter and the hunted; sometimes killing for food and at others to control pests. Nearly every day rabbits could be seen in the warrens, the young at play, adults feeding, all stopping at the slightest sound to sit upright and scan the fields with their eyes and long pointed ears; then, they were animals to watch and enjoy. But every Boxing Day, as well as in the harvest fields, Father and Jim assumed the mantle of huntsmen searching for food; the rabbits were their quarry, to be pursued, killed and ultimately eaten.

Over the years eating habits and hunting fashions changed considerably, but the essential drama of life and death continued. As a boy, Charlie had built brick sparrow traps for sparrow pie and Jim could remember, during hard winters, watching men using lark reels. When the snow was on the ground and after the finches and larks had flocked, farm labourers would unwind a length of cord from a reel and peg it firmly into the frozen snow. At intervals of every two or three inches horse hair snares were tied, with corn being sprinkled over them. The birds then settled to feed and scrap for food, and many would be caught by their feet in the slip knotted loops. The finches were released, and the larks were killed and sent to London where they were served up as delicacies in expensive hotels and restaurants.

Throughout the parish, predators other than man could be seen; creatures being hunted or preying on others so that life could continue. When it occurred in the garden with cats killing young blackbirds or thrushes, it did seem cruel and we would chase them, pelting them with stones. But with the truly wild, hunting seemed to contain a certain basic beauty, giving dignity to death; foxes on silent footpads testing the air for sound and scent, and approaching their victims with stealth and cunning. Sparrowhawks flying low over the hedgerows to hurl themselves at small birds, their talons tearing at flesh and their eyes flaming yellow, full of primitive anger. Patches of damp pigeon feathers, the dark stains of dry blood on grass, and the

abandoned carcasses of headless hens told how life was lost and gained. I sometimes felt sorrow for the victims, but never anger, and enjoyed the taste of rabbit with redcurrant jelly and stuffing balls, the same as everybody else.

Virtually any method of capturing rabbits was considered legitimate, with those not having guns usually resorting to the snare; poaching with them in private fields or setting them on common ground or along council ditches. The only trouble with snares was that they could never guarantee to catch the animal they were set for. Jim remembered an old land worker, who had once lived near the farm, setting a snare in the bottom of a ditch near the Warners Corner spinney, in what he took to be a hare run. Checking it one morning he saw animal movement and, assuming that he had been successful, he fell on the snare intending to kill his victim. Much to his surprise it was a fox that slashed his hands with panic-stricken chopping bites. The old man, not wanting to lose his unexpected prey tried to throttle it until all resistance stopped. He took the body out of the snare and laid it down while he studied his damaged hands. Having patched them up with his handkerchief, and feeling pleased with his efforts, he bent down to pick up the corpse by its brush, but it had gone, having quietly recovered and slunk off into the trees. Charlie's experience was slightly different, for he often set his three snares along the banks of the railway line; one morning he checked to see if he had caught a dinner to find that he had a ginger tom cat, a stoat and a hedgehog.

Numerous stratagems were also employed to get rid of rats; digging them out of hen house floors with the dogs close at hand to shake them and run their teeth along their backs, crushing nearly every bone in their bodies; and far more gruesome methods. Metal-sprung gin traps would be set behind sacks in the barn, poison would be laid outside holes and on the rafters, and both Jim and Charlie had special lethal schemes of their own. Jim's consisted of placing two bowls outside rat holes, one containing water, and the other a mixture of pig food and plaster of paris. The rats then ate the meal, quenched their thirst with water, and soon afterwards, he said, they died, with their insides set solid. Charlie's method was equally simple and was reserved for rats that made holes in cracked concrete floors.

He would find an old bottle, jar or pane of glass, smash it into minute pieces, and mix the splinters with cement. When the mixture was of the right consistency he would fill in the hole, levelling it off with the floor and leave it to harden; we imagined the entombed rats, with bleeding feet, dying as they deserved. None of these methods seemed cruel, for rats were a constant menace, gnawing holes in sacks, frightening us as they clawed along the wooden beams of the granary and old cow shed, killing young chickens and fouling the bins of corn.

The arrival of the hunt in the village with its hounds and horsemen also seemed entirely natural, for the foxes hunted without mercy and it seemed only right that they, in turn, should be hunted. When the hounds met at the Hoops, Miss Whitmell allowed us to stop work and led us out of the playground and into School Lane to watch as the huntsmen drank toasts, the whipper-in cracked his whip at straying dogs, and the hounds with cold noses, hot breath and long tongues, sniffed noisily around us. They were memorable occasions, with red coats in the pub yard, the beech trees turning the colour of old copper, the smell of horses, and the excited dogs anxious to be away. There were short fat men on long lean horses, men with top hats, half moon glasses, one with a monocle, and toothy women with refined voices, who looked as if they might suddenly neigh like their mounts. With a sharp 'tally-ho' on the horn and a crack of the whip, the entourage would move off, the hooves clattering on the metalled surface of the road, and several old countrymen with caps, long coats, and weather beaten faces following behind on their upright bicycles. All day long the occasional sound of baying hounds or the strains of the hunting horn would drift in on the wind, making us wonder what was happening and hope that the fox had got away. One afternoon it was quite clear that the hunt had been outwitted, for so many foxes were put up in the Jungle that the pack and the huntsmen were completely split, with small groups of lost and confused riders and dogs wandering through the village until well into the dusk.

Other hunts also visited the parish, including the Trinity Foot, whose kennels were near the rifle range and whose beagles were exercised by two huntsmen on bicycles along the deserted country roads early on summer mornings before most people were up. Shortly before 7 o'clock one fresh sunny morning I woke to hear the hounds returning, so I presumed, to their kennels, but something was wrong; they were in full cry, running out of control along the road. Some way in front, a golden labrador was running hard, heading for its home, its ears back, its tail between its legs, casting anxious glances

behind, then came the baying pack, and a long way to the rear came the huntsmen, pedalling frantically and shouting orders that every dog ignored. In winter the beagles' sport was more orthodox with green-coated undergraduates running with them over the ploughland and stubble in search of hares.

The drag hounds, too, were regular visitors, accompanied by black coated horsemen, to chase along the brook meadows in pursuit of a lone runner who dragged behind him a sack smelling of aniseed. With the course being carefully planned, and jumps being cut into some of the hedges, they galloped their predictable way, but although it lacked the spontaneity of fox hunting, there were still spills and mishaps. While Father and Jim were trimming and repairing a hedge at Lord's Bridge that had been damaged by a temporary gypsy encampment, a university rider, effusing inbred superiority endemic in some hunting families, arrogantly jumped the five-barred gate into the field. On landing the horse stopped abruptly but the rider kept going, doing a somersault in mid-air and, on hitting the ground, he rolled gently down a slope of the old gravel diggings, coming to rest sitting bolt upright in a puddle of stagnant water. Another time it was a horse that damaged itself and on arriving home from school we saw men trying to control it in Tinker's Field, so named because years before it had been a regular stopping place for travelling tinkers. The late afternoon was cold, damp, and misty, and the horse stood shivering, swaying, sometimes falling, and occasionally lashing out with its hind legs, sending those watching scampering out of range. It had damaged its back and could not be ridden or loaded into a horse box; eventually it was decided that nothing could be done and a vet was telephoned to put it down.

Father disliked many of those who hunted, but tolerated them on his land on condition that they repaired all the damage they caused to hedges and fences, and because our vet sometime rode with them. He had no objection to the beagles, as he was always notified of meets and he felt mild admiration for those who ran over the fields with the dogs, with clay clinging to and growing on their boots. He also welcomed the drag hounds, for each year they sent him free car passes to local point-to-point meetings. These he usually gave to the Gills Hill uncles, for with betting being on the same level as swearing and drinking, there was nothing to do in between races. In any case, we did go once, but at the first jump of the first race, a horse landed on its neck, which broke with a crack like a rifle shot, killing it instantly, and the incident put us off the sport even more.

But although hunting, ferreting, and snaring were popular, guns were the favourites of most people, whether wealthy landowners or simple working men. Father had three, including a double-barrelled twelve-bore shot gun, and a .22 rifle, which he used mainly on rats and rooks as they rooted up sprouting corn. Pigeons, too, were a major pest to be shot at as they descended onto the fields in noisily flapping grey clouds, or landed singly in the garden to eat the cabbages and brussels sprouts. As soon as John and I were considered old enough, he allowed us to use his small number one gun that he had used as a boy. It could shoot short range .22 bullets or French cartridges that showered shot at sparrows and starlings with flame coming from the end of the barrel and smoke curling up from the bolt. The cartridges varied greatly in quality, for sometimes the sparrows would fall stone dead, at others they would look surprised, ruffle their feathers and remain unmoved, and quite often the trigger would click and nothing further would happen.

Later Father gave John a .22 air rifle, and the farm became our stalking ground; hiding in the hen house, waiting for starlings to land at the free-range food troughs to blast at them, and searching for rats in the old cowshed and granary. We were told never to fire in the direction of people, or near the animals, but even so John managed to shoot Jim. He fired his rifle at a sparrow perching in front of the barn, the pellet missed, passed straight through the wooden wall and hit Jim in the middle of the back. It caused him no damage, but startled him, and he hurried out swearing and delivered John a stern lecture.

125

Our main enemies, however, for whom we reserved a special hatred, were the pike at Lord's Bridge, for they lived by eating the roach that we wanted to catch, but we could never catch them. They looked malignant and menacing and we considered it to be almost a public service to pepper them with shot. The meanness of pike was confirmed to me while I was fishing on a slight bend just before the entrance of Tit Brook. Amid the water lilies and the pointed leaves of arrowhead I caught a small dace, about an inch long, which I decided to leave on the hook in the hope that a pike would swallow it, hook and line as well. Twice the small fish was seized in the deep water well away from the bank, but both times it was quickly released. Thinking it unreasonable to expose it to risk and fear again I wound it in,

took it off the hook, and released it. As I was bending over, watching it drift slowly away with the current, a pike cruised in, gripped it between its jaws and sped away.

Our pike shooting season started in the early spring before the rushes grew to hide the shallow water and while the pike were still lethargic after spawning. We would shoot at them from the bank, aiming just below their bodies to allow for refracted light, and several were wounded and sent gulping to the bottom to die. Dicky hunted them with a bow and arrow, though he never hit one; once, however, while crossing the brook on a branch of fallen willow he saw an eel and shot it through the middle.

Jim, too, despite his war time experiences had a great affection for the gun, using an ancient twelve bore with a single barrel that seemed to expose him to far greater danger than the birds or animals at which it was pointed; sometimes he would borrow one of Father's. He was a good shot and a gun went with him almost everywhere, on the tractor at harvest time and at plough, and wherever Jim went with the gun, Peter the spaniel went too, plodding and sniffing just behind or else a long way in front.

Virtually anything that came into Jim's sights was considered to be game; crows, pigeons, partridges, rabbits and rooks, and no doubt Germans would have joined the list if Jim could have had his way. Once, while talking to Mother on the doorstep he saw a rat running between the thatch and wire of the granary roof and in mid-sentence he swung round and shot it with one swift movement. He also moved quickly on another occasion; it was on my birthday when I was due to have a party. Jim had borrowed Father's twelve bore and when he had finished with it he stood it in the corner of the living room, next to the door, in its usual place. The room filled up with my friends for food and games, and Jim went home. Two hours later, with the party in full swing, shortly after someone had just asked Mother if they could play with the gun, Jim suddenly burst in and grabbed it; while sitting at home in front of the fire he had remembered that for the first and only time in his life he had left it loaded.

His main enemies, when he had a gun in his hands, were pheasants, 'cunning old long tails', and he carried out a running feud with them, both in and out of season. Whenever they were within range and in season, he would shoot at them, whether they were flying, feeding in stubble, or perching up trees. Somehow the pheasants seemed to be aware of this and when Jim was ready with his gun, the birds were seldom to be seen. Consequently, as Jim and Peter walked over the fields during his dinner hour, there would usually be no signs of game; but when he was working without his gun, or could not stop to use it, the pheasants appeared to have assessed the situation and would feed nonchalantly, well within range. Talking about them afterwards Jim would take his cap off and scratch his head in frustration and if, out in the fields, a cock pheasant flew low over him when he was unprepared, he would mutter abuse at it and even stamp his feet.

When the shooting season came to an end the pheasants quickly seemed to realise that fact too. On 1 February they were still cautious and wary, but by 2 February they would walk about the fields openly, apparently unconcerned. 'Look at them,' Jim would mutter, 'strutting about there as if to say, 'Yes, here we are, and there's nothing you can damn well do about it'.' They were wrong though, for if a cock pheasant wandered too close to Jim, then the season never ended, and several times he quietly produced the .22 rifle, ostensibly to protect the growing corn as the birds were feeding.

Jim's was very much a love-hate relationship with the pheasants, and although in winter his favourite sight was to see a pheasant plummeting earthwards after he had shot it, during the summer he delighted in seeing hen birds skulking in the grass with their broods, or young chicks, smaller than blackbirds, flying low over the ears of corn. If, during hay and silage work, he cut a hen off her nest, he would carefully set the eggs under a broody farm hen, or bantam, in the hope that they would hatch and provide him with sport later in the year.

One year only a solitary cock bird survived this rearing, managing to avoid the large feet of his Rhode Island Red foster mother. We named him Charlie and became so attached to him that we clipped one of his wings and kept him in a hen run as a pet. Unfortunately, we failed to check the growth of new feathers and it was suddenly noticed that Charlie was missing; it was assumed that he had flown off. Rachael was very upset as he was her special pet, but Jim, who treated her almost as a daughter, assured her that he would be all right and would perhaps even come back. He was right, for two days later Charlie did come back. During his dinner hour Jim was taking his gun and Peter for a walk as usual, when the old dog stopped under an elm tree, looked up into it and began to bark. Jim looked up too and saw a cock pheasant perching in the lower branches. 'Ah, got you my beauty', he thought as usual, and killed it cleanly with one shot. Pleased at his success he hurried over to where it had fallen, only to find that it had one wing partially clipped; it was Charlie, and we ate him for Sunday dinner.

In general, pheasants enjoyed an almost privileged position in the eyes of most people in the village. On the dinner table they were generally acknowledged as tasting far better than cockerels, ducks, and turkeys, and in the fields they added colour to the stubble or the bare brown fields of winter; the cocks with their long tails and brilliant plumage, some, said to be of Chinese origin with conspicuous white collars. We enjoyed eating them, but disagreed with Father, who claimed that to achieve the best flavour they should be hung in a cool place for at least a fortnight and cooked as the skin was turning green. Whenever we had them or any game for dinner, the meat course was preceded by 'light pudding' with gravy, or 'blotting paper pudding' as we called it, a type of unsweetened sponge, that had been a traditional pudding in Mother's family for years; served before duck, partridges or jugged hare, it seemed ideal for preparing the appetite for the good things to follow.

Because of the unique affection in which the pheasants were held, and the intelligence which they were thought to possess, stories abounded of how to outwit and capture them. Many sounded far-fetched, but they were all said to be infallible and there was always someone who claimed to have seen even the most outrageous scheme succeed. Jim's particular favourite involved the use of burning sulphur beneath the trees where the pheasants roosted after dark. He claimed that as the birds inhaled the fumes they became dizzy and fell unconscious to the ground. Other methods were more simple, with many of them involving the use of raisins. One, said to be a favourite of poachers, made use of a trail of whisky-soaked raisins leading from a farmer's field to the poacher's garden. By the time the pheasants had travelled from private land to garden, they were supposed to be so drunk that they could neither fly nor stand. For those who could not afford whisky, some of the raisins could be fixed to fish hooks and lines, or stuck through with lengths of broom bristle which, if eaten by a pheasant, would stick in its throat and choke it.

Another cheap and unlikely way involved digging small holes and inserting in each one a paper cone, with corn at the bottom and glue on the sides. The pheasants were then said to peck at the corn, the glue stuck to their feathers, and the cone was lifted out like a large hat, completely covering the eyes and making the bird helpless. The most ingenious method, however, was also the cheapest, involving only hair from a horse's tail and a handful of grain. The tail was ruffled and combed into a large loose ball and the corn was sprinkled over it. When the pheasants scrapped for food, their wings and feet became tangled up in the hair and it was possible to walk over to them and pick them up. All the methods were apparently foolproof and Jim vowed that if he hadn't got a gun he would have put some of them into practice himself.

Uncle Roy and Uncle Cyril would not have approved of such unsporting devices, as they took their shooting very seriously, sometimes joining with neighbouring farmers in properly organised shoots, with beaters driving game towards a line of men with twelve bores. Uncle Cyril acted as his own gamekeeper, killing 'vermin' and rearing pheasants and partridge chicks in a home-made aviary. By the time I was in my early teens both uncles had grown to like organised shoots so much that they had joined a shooting syndicate that hired a large tract of Breckland forest. Often, on their way home after a good day's sport, they would call in to give Mother a brace of pheasants or to take advantage of Father's butchering, getting him to skin a deer, for which they would give him a joint of rich succulent venison.

Their tales of shoots in the forest with deer, pheasants, hares, jays, and various other birds and animals, filled us with interest and when they asked us if we would like to go with them to act as beaters for ten shillings a day, John, Michael and I jumped at the opportunity. Early on several Saturday mornings after that, during the shooting season, the Land-Rover arrived and we piled into the back, each with a stick and a packed lunch, looking forward eagerly to the day's activities.

Beyond Newmarket, with its strings of exercising race horses, the country gradually changed, the soil lightened, in places almost to the colour of sand, Scotch pines bordered the fields, there were patches of heathland covered with dead bracken, brown and flattened by wind and rain, and then forest began; blocks of dark pines, scrubland with thorns and silver birches, and areas of bog and marsh, dissected by small, icy streams. Past a garage, whose back yard was littered with the battered shells of large American cars from nearby air bases, the Land-Rover swung off the main road and drove into a small clearing beside a gamekeeper's cottage; we clambered out to join the other beaters, mainly boys, but also local men wanting to earn the adults' wage of £1. The guns stood in groups, talking, and slotting cartridges into their belts as they waited for late-comers.

When all was ready, some of the guns drove off to wait for us at a prearranged rendezvous; we beaters formed a long line and the day began. Our job was to force the game to break cover, so that it could be shot by those guns still with us, or driven forward to those waiting ahead; as we walked we hit the tree trunks or undergrowth with our sticks, and made various shooing noises to drive the game on. At each ride, a forest track between the blocks of trees, we waited for the stragglers to get into line and then we pushed forward again through the next plantation. Most of the trees were half-mature pines, with their lower branches trimmed and left to rot, making progress extremely difficult at times; but it provided ideal cover for the pheasants which, in turn, led to abundant sport. There were other trees too, blocks of large Douglas firs and small areas of tall Scotch pines, with spreading beds of bramble below, that we had to wade through. Occasionally there were breaks of heath, with hares running straight and fast, and always there were the whistles of command to the dogs and the firing of guns.

The forest was a fascinating place, with the distinctive smell of conifers heavy in the air and the crisp sound of fallen pine needles and dead bracken crunching underfoot. Early in the season, puff balls and scarlet flycap toadstools with their deadly beauty grew in the damp and dark beneath the pines, patches of snowberries flourished in the scrub, and throughout the day there was the promise of the unexpected.

Jays cried out angrily whenever they were disturbed, red squirrels fled along the branches to the safety of their dreys, feral golden pheasants with their plumage of fiery oranges and reds flew the gauntlet of the guns and, with crashing undergrowth and the thudding of hurried hooves, deer ran for safety to break through the slowly closing net of men and dogs. Men shouted 'over' as pheasants approached the guns, and in the woods and marshes woodcock were often flushed, winging low and fast in tight, zig-zagged flight. In addition to being planted with forest, the whole area was a frost and snow trap, and when hoary white settled over the wooded scene, sound travelled far through the clear cold air, black ice crept thinly over the streams, and after the gunfire snow would be sprinkled with drops of warm blood.

Both uncles were accurate shots and easy to get on with, but some of their companions varied as much as the dogs they took with them.

One short, fat man almost barked like his retriever, ordering beaters into line with booming shouts of command and usually picking on Michael because of his height: 'Oi Lofty come here', or 'where's Lofty? I've got a special job for you, come over here', and he would give him all the worst terrain to walk over. In fact, he made almost as much noise with his mouth as he did with his gun, for he invariably fired both barrels at whatever he saw, regardless of how close the victim was to him. His manners and marksmanship contrasted sharply with those of another gun who was tall, upright, and quiet; he never expected a beater to go where he could not go himself and he usually killed with one clean shot.

One of the other guns spent most of his day shouting abuse at his dog; his vocabulary was that of the barrack-room and his accent that of the officer's mess. He had two dogs, a spaniel and a labrador, neither of them took the slightest notice of him and disappeared into the distance at every pheasant or hare they scented, barking excitedly as they went. Every few minutes he would blow his whistle and bawl: 'Monty, Monty....Rex, come here you bastard.....Monty, Monty, where are you, you bugger you,' and as his throat became hoarse he lubricated it with the contents of a brandy flask, steadily becoming even noisier.

The beaters kept themselves very much to themselves, although it was noticeable that several of the older men seemed to know the woods far better than they liked to admit, and knew where the pheasants were likely to be found and where the deer spent their days. A local boy, several years my junior, was also something of an oddity, for he openly swore, even when adults were within hearing, and he smoked cigarettes and a pipe with the full approval of his grandfather, who also attended the shoots. He thought it most strange that we rarely smoked, and would only do so if we had peppermints to suck afterward to hide the smell of tobacco.

When pheasants were shot, we would compete with the dogs to pick them up, and those that were only wounded we killed by hitting them hard over the head with our sticks. After each drive the game was thrown into a Land-Rover, and another was soon started. On we would go, tripping over branches, crossing streams on single planks of wood, jumping ditches with boggy banks while trying not to lose our boots, and getting caught up in briers. Coming from a small plantation to a stretch of heath and marshland during one cold morning's shoot, a most chilling incident occurred. A pheasant was shot and spiralled down beyond a wire mesh fence that had a barbed top strand. As usual one of the labradors went to retrieve it, a particularly fine and friendly dog, but on trying to jump the fence it slipped, a barb sank deep into its flesh, and it hung suspended in the air, struggling and yelping, as if caught by its stomach. After a few seconds it fell to the ground and continued its chase apparently unhurt, to return to its master soon afterwards, wagging its tail, with the pheasant in its mouth. It was then noticed that something had been left hanging on the barbed wire, and on inspection it was found that practically the whole of the dog's penis was still impaled on the barb. Later in the day after it had visited a vet, and been strapped up the dog returned, looking very sorry for itself.

Once, too, a stoat with its winter coat of white ermine and black-tipped tail was cornered in a pile of wood. Its eyes were wild, with a look of inborn ferocity, and its lithe body darted in and out of the stacked posts and poles to evade the dogs and prodding sticks. Finally Uncle Cyril shot it, its fierce beauty was stilled and its once spotless coast was flecked with oozing red.

By midday, after three hours of continuous beating, we were always thirsty and tired, and crates of beer and cider were produced for us, or we would get free drinks in the public bar of a local pub while the guns were in the lounge bar drinking and discussing the morning's sport. Many of us were well under age and several times, by the afternoon drives, my tiredness had gone and the cider led me to stumble merrily through the woods with my legs feeling unusually light. At the end of the day the game was laid out in a long line, pheasants, partridges, woodcock, rabbits, hares, and usually a deer; it was then divided up into more or less equal heaps and the guns drew lots to decide who was having what. The local beaters were paid off, and we joined the others at an old inn for mugs of hot tea and rounds of buttered toast.

Gradually, however, I began to feel uneasy about the shoots, for they seemed far divorced from the situation of Jim and Father shooting the odd rabbit or pheasant for dinner, and there often seemed to be much needless killing and suffering. At a shoot over the fields near Gills Hill a dog found an old lame hare that had been injured on a previous occasion, and as the dog went to kill it, it screamed with the piercing shrieks of a suffering child. But the incidents in the forest were the ones that really saddened me. Normally, I was excited every time I saw a red squirrel, for at home, in the spinney, and occasionally in the garden we only saw greys. But one morning, as we rested after a particularly strenuous drive, a squirrel could be seen high up above us, among the branches of a mature Scotch pine, it was almost skipping from branch to branch stopping every now and then to look down at us or to preen. All at once, for no apparent reason, a tall man with a moustache and the air of a country magistrate, took aim and fired. The squirrel thudded to the ground dead: 'Oh dear, I thought it was a grey,' he mumbled as disapproving glances were cast at him; but we all saw, well before he shot, that from the tip of its long bushy tail, to the points of its tufted ears, it was a dark chestnut red.

On another occasion, high up in the cold, limpid air, two small ducks flew past and direct over the trees, heading for the washes or an inland lake, their ancestral wintering place. Two shots rang out and they, too, fell dead. It seemed a tragedy to me; they were teal, whose glossy feathers and small fine lines, perfected through centuries of rapid streamlined flight, deserved a better end. Later on in the same day I chased after a wounded woodcock and caught it, much to the satisfaction of the gun who had fired, for as their flight made them difficult to hit, it meant that he could claim £1 from all his companions. It was a beautiful bird with mottled brown plumage, the colour of fallen forest leaves, soft brown eyes and a long probing beak. As I held it by the neck it seemed to be asking for release, healing and freedom. I struck it over the head with my stick, blood welled into its eyes and red tears formed as if it was crying in real sorrow; I struck it again harder, and it twitched violently in a spasm of death.

But it was the fate of the deer that really disturbed me; small roe deer with delicate features, pointed ears, alert eyes, thick fawn coats and flanks of brilliant white; they had a charm and grace that gave poetry to movement. When alarmed, the bucks would sometimes give a low, loud bark of warning, they would crash through the undergrowth, glide through the line of beaters and guns, leaping high for greater speed and clearing the forest fences with consummate ease. Most got away, but the unfortunate few were sprayed with shot, rarely being killed outright, but stumbling to a halt, maimed by lead pellets, their eyes filling with fear. Some managed to hobble on to hiding places, where death came slowly as pain and gangrene steadily spread. Several times dead deer were found, and one, still alive, was unable to move. Its eyes were glazed and sightless, its body blown and hard, full of gases from the rotting wounds, and the only sign of life came from its laboured breathing.

Wounded deer usually fell and sat as if resting, waiting for another cartridge to be discharged. The son of one of the regular guns was allowed to shoot one afternoon and he hit a deer. The animal stumbled and fell with countless pellets lodged in its side, then it sat quietly in the grass, its head held up, looking meek and apprehensive. The boy, three years older than me, advanced under the watchful eye of his father to within twelve yards of where it lay, took careful aim and pulled the trigger. The deer rolled over, half its head disintegrated and disappeared, leaving behind blood, brain and white bone. 'I've killed my first deer,' he kept repeating afterwards, but he stayed well away from the half headless body.

The worst death occurred after a deer had been wounded and two beaters insisted that it would be a waste of a cartridge to shoot again; instead they proposed to slit its throat. The gun agreed and left them to it, leaving also the deer sitting passively, looking completely normal, but with its legs paralysed. It looked so calm that it was difficult to think of it either as a wild creature, or as a pest, and I longed to take it home to try and cure it and have it as a pet. The youths then set to work, one roughly held its head on the ground with his foot, the other took a small penknife from his pocket and stuck it into the animal's neck. The deer was now terrified and struggled desperately, but with its legs useless and its head held firm it could not escape the blade's cutting, thrusting, and probing. Hardly any blood trickled out, and the youth, his stomach for the job rapidly turning, hacked violently with the knife, severing the windpipe and cutting a gaping hole in the throat. The deer was gasping frantically for air, breathing directly through the ugly wound and open pipe; the youths kicked it, jumped up and down on its neck, but still it lived. An old beater finally pushed them out of the way. 'Come here, give me the knife,' he muttered, and cut cleanly and deeply, severing the jugular veins; blood streamed out onto the grass and life quickly flowed away. I was sickened and decided never to go shooting again.

CHAPTER 8

Feathers and Feet

———

It was not strange that I should react so against shooting; in fact the real surprise was that I went on those trips into the Breckland forests for so long. For in general we lived in harmony with the creatures around us, whether they were shut in yards or sties on the farm, or wild along the hedgerows. All day and night the sights and sounds of birds and animals mingled with rest, work, and play, becoming an integral part of everyday life. Anxious cows would wake us, bellowing after being separated from their calves, cocks began to crow before first light, grunts and squeals came intermittently from the pig yard, and the dogs and cats relied on us for affection and security.

But those in the wild influenced us just as much as the livestock on the farm; at the rhythmic sibilance of lazy wing beats we would run from the house to watch wild swans fly over head, usually mutes, alone, or with a mate, but in the spring and autumn there were others, as white as the ice they left behind each year in the Arctic tundra. Tawny and barn owls hooted eerily on moonlit nights, little owls or 'sceechers' perched on the top of telegraph poles, to be silhouetted by the lights of passing cars and, very occasionally on rough autumn evenings, ragged skeins of Canada geese could be seen flying low against the wind returning to a gravel pit several miles away. Fieldfares and redwings came into the garden to eat fallen apples during times of winter scarcity, and each spring we waited eagerly for the return of the swallows and the first call of the cuckoo.

The swallows came back every year to perch on the electric cable strung between the house and the barn, crossing the pig yard on the way, and they nested in the garage, the old stable, the tractor shed, sometimes in the hen houses, and in the barn as well. Their eager twittering and joyful flight made them welcome and we would watch

them collecting mud from the edge of puddles in the farmyard, and later we would sit
quietly in the car as parent birds flew into
the garage with beaks brimful of insects to
feed to their ever hungry young. At the
end of long summer days, when dusk and
dawn drifted slowly almost together, they
would fly high in the pale pastel blue of
evening skies, and above them, still higher,
screeching swifts would rush on jet black
scimitar wings, celebrating the freedom of

the air. Some years the cuckoos hardly ever seemed to stop calling,
from the spinney, the Jungle and the trees near the Leys, and they
only quietened after all the available nests had been temporarily
stolen and the females had laid their eggs.

Hedgehogs provided us with more earthbound charm; in winter
we found them hibernating in piles of leaves and straw and in summer lone individuals would come into the garden or farmyard at
dusk, searching for food. If we were feeling benevolent we would put
a saucer of milk nearby, which they would drink after we had gone,
but when we were feeling
more inquisitive and
found one near the house
during the day, we would
carefully pick it up, curled
in a tight, defensive, prickly
ball, to drop it into a water
butt and make it swim. On
hitting the water each one
would uncurl immediately and
swim strongly, their short legs work-
ing quickly and their pig-like snouts well above water. Jim told us
that their ducking never did them any harm as they were always
lousy and it was the only way to get rid of their fleas, but however
hard we peered through their matted spines, we never saw any signs
of parasitic life. Sometimes we swam them in an old bath tub, where
we also kept newts, transferred from the village pond; they were

colourful lizard-like creatures, that quickly escaped, and sometimes reappeared days later, searching for insects on an overgrown rockery in the garden.

All these seemed to be as much a part of the farm as we were, and because of our attachment to many of them, it was inevitable that we should have some special pets. Bantams roamed the garden at will, Muscovy ducks were everywhere and in winter flew on new flight feathers in wide circles around the buildings, sometimes perching on the roofs of nearby houses. One fell down a chimney, causing smoke-filled rooms in a neighbour's house, and was not discovered until the sweep dislodged it during the summer. He visited practically all the houses in the village, cycling round on his bicycle with his rods and brushes strapped to the bar, towing a small trailer for carrying bags of soot; when he took his pipe from his mouth and smiled, his teeth gleamed white against his soot covered face, as did his bald head when he removed his cap.

Over the years hundreds of chickens arrived, to grow into hens, lay eggs, and finally to be served up on various dinner plates. When compared with the ducks they were stupid birds, with little character and no sense; all except one, Henrietta. For some reason, even as a chicken, she spurned the company of her own kind, refusing to be shut in the hen house at night, spending her days scrapping around the back door and feeding in the barn on spilt corn and meal. On hot days she would make a dust bath in the drive and if the door of the house was left open she would walk in and stroll about the living room and kitchen, hoping to find crumbs. When the rest of the hens were shut up to lay, she remained free, perching at night in the barn where foxes could not reach her, and long after the others of her batch had gone, she still walked enquiringly

139

into the house, her head cocked slightly to one side as if asking for permission to enter, and her life lasted its full and natural span, which was well over ten years.

Guinea fowl arrived one day, in a sack, as Father had always wanted some. They were in the main white-spotted slate grey birds, shy, dainty, smaller and more delicate than hens, and fast running like partridges; when courting or content they would call out a melodic 'Come back, come back', but when disturbed, or upset by the approach of strangers they would scold, with harsh grating cries that made them as effective as any watch dog. After two days shut up to get acclimatized, they were released from a small shed into the hen run. No sooner were they out than they flew over the road and into the fields. We chased them in vain and had to wait for nightfall, when they went to roost in the elm trees by the recreation ground. They were finally caught with the aid of a ladder and bright torches, dazzling them as they perched and we grabbed their feet. They were welcome additions to the farm and were a feature of it for several years, until their numbers gradually dwindled and the last remaining bird died of old age, safely shut with the hens in a deep litter shed. Unfortunately, just as we liked them, so, too, did foxes and whenever one visited the hen runs at night and found guinea fowl and hens skulking in the long grass, the guinea fowl were always the ones to be taken.

Mother had always wanted us to have something larger; a pony like the one Mr Holben had given her, but as Father considered them to be too expensive, they compromised and gave us a friendly grey donkey, old when he came to us, but for some reason he seemed to get no older. 'Ah well, you never see a dead donkey,' Jim informed us, having seen many that had seemed to live indefinitely. Father disagreed, for when he had been a boy his donkey had died after eating the leaves of a yew tree, but Jim insisted that such a stupid beast could not be counted.

We had proper reins and a saddle for Neddy, and before we grew too big for him we enjoyed trying to ride. Normally he would trot reluctantly, walk only after much persuasion, lifting his back legs high, as if over invisible obstacles, but usually he would just stand still and refuse to move. When he was not being ridden, he lived with the cows, grazing with them in the fields, and whenever he saw a horse or pony pass by he would bray, slowly at first, gradually speeding up. His wish for more amiable company was satisfied when a retired army colonel and his family moved into the thatched cottage on the Leys, for they brought a pony with them and asked Father if it too could graze with the cows. The donkey became so attached to it that whenever the colonel's wife or daughter went riding he would stand sadly at the gate, waiting patiently for them to return. In fact the donkey was so affected by loneliness that several years later when the colonel, his family, and two ponies left the village, they took the donkey with them, and Jim was again proved right.

During his stay, the colonel added a dash of military splendour to the village, playing an active part in village life and quickly getting elected onto the parish council, which, when he became chairman, he ran almost like an army tribunal. When the weather was hot he wore long khaki shorts, that hung down to just below his knees, and they in turn were met by matching long khaki socks, which hid his white skin almost completely. He was extremely fond of country life and at Christmas time he gave presents of horse manure to some of his neighbours as a sign of appreciation. His children joined in with the rest of us, sharing our liking for animals and once, while out in the fields, they found a young leveret. It flourished with them, until one day it gnawed through their television lead and was electrocuted.

We had a long procession of pets, which became almost complete members of the household, and whenever one died there was always mourning, with small graves being dug in the garden, marked by a daffodil or a rose. The first one to upset me was Judy, an old

Labrador who hated rats, loved children, and taught Peter how to follow a gun. She grew old gracefully and died peacefully, near one of the lych gates in the front garden. The hamster, too, was a loss the first time he died, going cold, stiff, and lifeless. He was old and his end came as no surprise, so I took his body out of the cage and left it for Father to bury. By the time he arrived to carry out his task he could find no body, just the hamster completely normal, warm, moving, and full of life. It died twice more after that, with our sorrow diminishing each time; on the last occasion we left him stiff and cold for well over a week until we were quite sure that he would be resurrected no more.

Rachael's pet pig, Billy, had a more predictable end, for she looked after him from the time he was a piglet, rejected by his mother, until he had grown into a fat and gluttonous porker. In fact, so well did she feed him that he developed stomach ruptures; but it made no difference to either his diet or his greed. Each time Rachael walked by his pen he grunted in appreciation, but alas, as both he and his appetite grew, he could be kept no longer, and one morning he was quietly taken to market.

Of all the pets we had, those taken from the wild and tamed were the ones we regarded with the most affection. First there were two baby rabbits taken from a rabbit hole in Warners Corner while ferreting. The ferret had killed the rest of the family and by the time they were dug out, there were just the two left alive; blind, helpless bundles of warm fur that I carried home in the inside of my windcheater. We kept them in a cardboard box on the Aga, and fed them every few hours with milk administered from a fountain pen filler. After a few days, their eyes opened and they became so lively that their box could not hold them. They would run about the kitchen, sit up on their hind legs, their noses twitching and their whiskers quivering, hoping for a piece of carrot, or some other titbit. They reminded us of rabbits in Walt Disney's cartoon film of *Bambi*, but unlike that film, their story did not have a happy ending, for one afternoon they jumped out of their box while a cat was in the kitchen, and later I sorrowfully buried what was left of them in the garden.

Soon afterwards, we did have more luck with another young rabbit which Father caught in the brook meadows. He had seen a family of baby rabbits playing near some brambles, where they were so absorbed in their game that they did not notice him slowly approaching. When he got near enough he dived forward and put his hat over one; we called it Thumper. It quickly became extremely tame and, as a special concession, each Sunday evening it was allowed to run loose in the drawing room. On one such evening, when the wind was still cold enough to make a fire necessary, it sat on the hearth rug looking into the flames. Then, without warning it suddenly jumped onto the white hot embers at the back of the fire, before leaping out again and running round the room stamping its hot back feet on the carpet; fortunately the only damage done was to its tail, which was slightly singed. It grew to full maturity and after two years of captivity finally regained its freedom when it gnawed through its hutch and was last seen disappearing into a hedge alongside the garden.

Like Father before us, we also had a young jackdaw one summer, taken from its nest just as its feathers were appearing and fed on a diet of bread and milk. It was a friendly bird, with soot-black feathers on its body, and a head of steely grey, giving it the appearance of having the wisdom and the wig of a High Court judge. After it had learned to fly, it visited several neighbouring gardens, and on seeing us searching for it, would call out 'Jack, Jack', in recognition. It became so tame that it seemed that cats or cars would eventually kill it and so, to limit its wanderings, we cut one of its wings. This had the desired effect, until, while perching on a garden fork it tried to fly and fell fluttering into a clump of bindweed where it was caught up on the tentacle-like stems and the more it struggled, the tighter it was held. Later that evening after it had been found and untangled, our favourite pet died of shock.

We had two other wild birds and both of them had strange ends; one mysterious and the other sad. The first bird arrived after a telephone call from a neighbour, asking if we had lost a duck, because he had one on his lawn, washing itself under a garden hose. It did not belong to us, being completely black, except for a small triangle of yellow on its bill, quite unlike our own Muscovies. Although not knowing what it was, Father collected it, hoping that it would join our ducks. On getting it home it soon became obvious that it was far from well, however, for it experienced difficulty when trying to walk and it seemed very weak. Consequently we put it for shelter in the engine room at the end of the house, where an old engine periodically sucked water from our bore hole into a tank in the roof.

We had no idea what to feed it on, or what it was, so Father telephoned the Royal Society for the Prevention of Cruelty to Animals in the hope that some advice would be forthcoming; he was told that the only duck it could possibly be was an Indian Runner, a ponderous, domesticated duck, and that it patently was not. Knowing that our ducks were happiest when sifting sludge through their beaks at the edge of puddles, Father made a similar substance from a mixture of milk and porridge oats. The bird thrived on this soggy, cold, raw substance, quickly regaining its strength, to waddle up and down the lawn and flap its still weak wings. As it became stronger we put a wire roof over the old bath, then empty of newts to let it swim and wash. On being put in for the first time it showed obvious signs of joy, spraying itself by beating its wings on the water, then diving and staying immersed for what seemed like minutes on end, stirring up the algae and mosquito larvae from the bottom. Its progress was so rapid we decided that within a few days it would be strong enough for release and we would let it out to fly back to the far off waters from where it had obviously come.

By this time John was a scout, and the day before we planned to let the duck go, Father took us all to the sea where John was under canvas; on our return in the evening, the duck had vanished. Part of the mystery, but not all, was solved by Jim who told us that while we were away an R.S.P.C.A. inspector had arrived wanting to see the duck. Not knowing what had been arranged earlier on the telephone, Jim took him to the engine room, whereupon the bird had been caught, put in a box and taken away. Father was mystified and angry; he had not told anyone to collect it, especially as it had fully recovered and was ready for release. He telephoned the organisation again, but could get no explanation and was eventually told that the duck had been taken to the University Botanical Gardens and let loose on a pond. Those at the gardens knew of no such story, and so what happened to our friendly black duck we never found out. Several years later I noticed a similar bird, stuffed and still, looking out from a glass case in a museum. It was a Common Scoter, a diving duck from cold northerly waters, and no doubt ours had been blown inland by gales, exhausted; all I hoped as I spotted it among the rows of stuffed birds, was that ours was not the one that stared blankly back at me.

The other bird's end was all too clear to see, yet all we could do was watch helplessly. One summer afternoon Mrs Walder, who, with her husband, lived in our old cottage and loved the quiet and simple pleasures of country life, came to tell us that a young owl, unable to fly, was at the bottom of her garden. She was worried in case a cat or dog should get it, and to put her at ease, Socrates was brought in to become another member of our family. He was a beautiful bird, a tawny owl, with large, dark eyes, a hooked beak that he clicked in warning when approached, light brown plumage, a mixture of feathers and down, softer that anything Mother had ever touched before, and powerful talons, that at first struck at us in anger, but later, as fear left him, enabled him to perch on my bare forearm without marking my skin.

He quickly settled in and was the centre of attraction whenever anybody called to see us. When perching on the back of a chair in the kitchen, his head would slowly and smoothly turn through one hundred and eighty degrees and, unless his feet could be seen, it was not always obvious which way he was, in fact, facing. As he grew bigger, we let him perch on the rustic rose arches surrounding the back lawn, and no sooner was he settled, motionless, as if in deep meditation then chaos occurred, for he was mobbed by a host of small birds. Sparrows, starlings, blackbirds, thrushes, robins, and blue-tits flew angrily around him, crying out shrilly in alarm, and swallows swooped low overhead.

After a few days, when it became clear to them that he was different from those owls that flew at dusk, the birds took no further notice of him. We had no difficulty in getting him to feed, for the

145

daughter of George Disbrey worked in a university laboratory and brought us dead mice that even Mother cut up and fed to him. Fur, feet and bones were all swallowed, and later he brought them up again as small pellets of waste. To enable him to pellet properly when no mice were available, we fed him with pieces of beef wrapped in feathers.

Gradually feathers replaced infant down and we put him in a cage to prevent him flying away. Captivity and confinement were totally alien, and his tawny features etched with dark streaks, seemed entirely out of place within the confines of four small walls. As a result, we decided that the only proper thing to do was to let him go. Close to his time of release, misfortune struck when Mother, who had resumed teaching at a small school in Cambridge, took him to show her class, but held him too tightly to prevent him from flying away and he broke a leg. Fortunately, several years earlier I had been caught up in a craze for collecting plaster-cast impressions of bird footprints; it had quickly passed, but had left us with nearly half a stone of plaster of Paris powder. Consequently, Father decided to set Socrates' leg in a plaster bandage, and six weeks later the bones had knitted perfectly and the leg was back to normal.

Some time later, remembering his success with the owl, Father applied a similar bandage to the leg of a cockerel, and again after six weeks the bird could walk almost normally. The recovery was not quite complete however, for somehow Father had set the foot the wrong way round, a fact that was not noticed until the plaster was removed. As a result one foot pointed to the front and the other pointed to the back, and the unfortunate bird left footprints as if two one-legged cockerels had passed each other, hopping in different directions.

Once he had recovered, Socrates quickly learnt to fly and he flew confidently about the living-room, his wings silent and his talons sure. We finally decided that he was strong enough to go and that his deceptive beauty would only reach its full potential in the wild where he belonged. So, pleased with his progress, we again let him perch on the rose arches, completely free. After a few moments of apparent contemplation he quietly flew off, over the orchard, towards the garden from where he had originally come. We watched him go, until his flight took him higher, to the top of a tall ash tree, where, we assumed he would wait for nightfall and food.

Much to our surprise, the following morning he was still there and there he remained for several days, just sitting, with eyes staring vacantly ahead. At night too, he did not move, and the beam of our large lantern picked him out still perching, never hunting or feeding. It was clear that captivity had removed his wildness and he was incapable of fending for himself; it was also clear that if he was not recaptured he would starve. Whenever we stood near the tree, calling his name, he just observed us placidly, but our ladders were too short and the branches were too thin to get anywhere near him.

Inevitably, one morning he was gone; Father assumed that he was dead, but I persuaded myself that he was still alive, that he had flown, killed, and eaten, and was hiding up for the day like any normal owl. Two hours later we were both proved wrong, for Father spotted him perching in a hedge. He tried to catch him, but Socrates flew off, losing height steadily, until he came to rest on a decaying wooden cart in the farm-yard. There he offered no resistance, he clicked his beak feebly but there was no other signs of wildness or struggle. His plumage had lost its lustre, his eyes were sunken in their large sockets, and his bones felt like fragile twigs protruding from his emaciated body. He was so weak that he made no more attempts to fly, and even standing became an effort. To make matters worse he refused all food, and later that afternoon I found him dead in his cage, his meat untouched. Like a flower that had suddenly withered and died, his beauty had just wasted away; I went up to my room heartbroken.

All these pets I found fascinating, but I was never completely satisfied, for what I wanted more than anything else, even before I had seen one, was a fox. Foxes intrigued me; Jim muttered about them, but had a grudging admiration for their cunning, Miss Whitmell read us stories of their exploits, and an elderly great aunt gave me a small book that took me into the world of Brer Rabbit and Brer Fox.

Consequently, the day I saw my first fox on the brook bank, I hurried home to tell Father and Mother, and it made me want a cub even more. I saw several foxes after that, in the brook meadows and in the Jungle, and each time the thrill was just as great as the time before.

On an evening in early summer when I was wandering through the brook meadows with the sun still warm and the long grass swirling in waves and eddies in the wind, I froze in my tracks as I saw a fox some two hundred yards away. The wind was right, carrying my scent away, and I remained motionless. It was a fine animal, a deep russet red, with a prominent white tip to its tail, in the peak of condition. Holding its nose aloft briefly it trotted off towards an isolated cluster of small bushes, I followed, tense, my heart thumping with excitement. Every time the fox stopped, I stood motionless, and when it reached the bushes and began looking into the branches, sometimes standing on its hind legs as if searching for nests, I cautiously drew nearer. When I was within ten yards of it I could contain myself no more. 'Got you,' I shouted, to see its reaction. It looked round in alarm, almost in disbelief, its ears flattened, and it fled to the brook where only the scolding blackbirds knew its line of retreat.

At the far end of Warners Corner, along an old drift, and among numerous rabbit holes, was a much larger hole, with sand and gravel scraped out in an untidy heap around its main entrance. This, Father told me, was a fox's earth, and every spring and summer the growing corn nearby was flattened by romping cubs, and picked hen carcasses and chewed bones littered the area. One year after much pressure from us, he agreed that we could have a cub, and with Tom Murkin, John, a sack, a gun and two spades, we went to dig out the earth, which in early April was bound to hold young. John and I were both excited, we had a cage and bowls for

food all ready, and had told our friends of the pet we intended to capture.

Arriving at the holes we were immediately dismayed, for it was obvious that somebody had been there before us; the earth had not been dug, instead its two entrances had been sealed, as had those of several rabbit holes. Tom Murkin cleared some of the soil away, and just inside found some white powder and the pungent smell of gas. It seemed that we had arrived too late, but as the gassing was recent, Father and Tom agreed that the young might still be alive. Looking into the hole they guessed where to dig, hoping to reach the end of the earth before the gas. They estimated exactly right and quickly dug through the roof where the earth ended, and there, with their noses pressed to the wall at the furthest point from the entrance and the creeping smell of gas, were three small cubs huddled together; but we had lost the race for they were all dead, with the one at the bottom still warm.

As a result we never had a fox, although my fascination for them remained, as did my habit of wandering through the meadows, alone, with the dog, or with Chris, always hoping for another fleeting glimpse. In April 1966, the chance came that I had wanted years earlier, for when strolling through the Jungle with Chris, the Sunday before Easter, a fox, disturbed by our voices, startled us by jumping from a hole in the trunk of an elm some eight feet from the ground. Jim had told me many times before tales of foxes hiding up for the day in willows, climbing up their rotting trunks to crawl into a hole or hollow, but I had remained sceptical. Now I believed him and climbed up to the hole, which was dark and fusty, but I could see nothing inside. Just as I was about to jump down, Chris, who was looking through a connecting crack lower down, noticed movement. Looking in again I, too, saw signs of life through the gloom and, disappearing head-first into the hole I felt fur and brought out three dark cubs, covered with soft, woolly fur, their eyes still shut and their ears curled up; they looked more like Alsatian puppies than foxes. Two we put back inside, and by the next day, the vixen had moved them to a less accessible home. One we kept, naming him Cassius.

Difficulties immediately set in, for unlike the rabbits years earlier, we could not get the young cub to feed from a fountain pen filler.

Instead, with much embarrassment, I had to purchase a 'Baby Dolly Set' from a large multiple store, which included a small rolling pin and a plastic potty, just to get a feeding bottle that he would accept. He quickly took to it, gulping down the sweetened milk greedily. His eyes gradually opened, his ears uncurled, and the only problem to remain was the constipation that set in with his change of diet. That, too, was eventually solved by occasionally lacing his milk with syrup of figs.

Our labrador, Rinty, tolerated the new arrival patiently, allowing his paws to be chewed and his tail pulled, and when he died suddenly after eating half a bucket full of slug bait, Cassius and the new puppy that arrived played together as if they were from the same litter. Normally the cub would stay in the garden, but twice he wandered over the road into Tinkers Field where he got lost in the growing corn. Both times, as Mother stood calling him, a ripple appeared far off among the green stems and a frail whimper gradually moved towards her until he greeted her with obvious delight.

As he grew older, he was instantly attracted by all movement, leaves swaying in the wind, bees flying from flower to flower, cats, which he would attack playfully, brush first to avoid their claws, and inevitably, hens. Hens seemed almost to hypnotise him, and while they were much larger than he was, he would stalk them in the hen

run, always maintaining a respectful distance. By the time he was half grown, they seemed less intimidating, and after stalking one moulting fowl for half an hour, he finally pounced, seizing the startled bird by the tail. The hen squawked in alarm and tried to run, dragging Cassius reluctantly behind; suddenly release came, the hen was free, and Cassius was left, looking confused with a mouthful of feathers.

He learnt quickly after that, and the next time he attacked he made no mistake, holding a hen by the neck. This meant that whenever he was not being watched over he had to be chained up and released in the evenings when he and the puppy would chase over the lawns and garden. Although we failed to house-train him, he was allowed into the living-room quite often, where he developed a keen liking for sponge cake, chocolate and hazel nuts. If none were given to him he would search the room, jumping onto the side-board from a standing position, and landing so lightly on all fours that no ornament would be knocked over and no scratch would be made on the polished wood. On walks he always avoided water, when pheasants were flushed he would try to leap into the air in pursuit, and he enjoyed sniffing large thistles, in much the same way as dogs smell lamp-posts.

But however much we handled him, fussed him, and had him in the house, we could not curb his liking for ducks, and hens, and several summer mornings we woke to the cries of fowl in distress. Then, as pyjama and wellington boot clad figures chased him through the dew-soaked grass and horse-radish, he skipped and danced ahead, always just out of reach, thoroughly enjoying himself. When this happened we had to let the puppy out too, for he also enjoyed these early morning games, catching Cassius by the brush and holding him until we could make him secure once more. If pulled from a hen that he was eating, he would squeal angrily, sounding like a pig, and once he ripped my finger open in rage, but normally he only killed for the pleasure of seeing feathers flutter. By the autumn he had killed so many hens that I wrote out a small cheque for Father as conscience money.

Sadly, like the pets of childhood, his end came sooner than anticipated, for as the mating calls of wild foxes could be heard at night, coming from the direction of the spinney and the brook, he became increasingly restless, sniffing the air and wanting to be free. One night he broke loose again, dragging his chain behind him and disappearing completely. The following day I walked along the hedgerows of the brook meadows calling his name, but we saw him no more. He ran free for several miles, so we were told later, and after a light fall of snow a farmer followed strange tracks, as if an animal had been trailing a gin trap, which led to a shallow hole among the roots of a tree. Not knowing what had caused them he put the barrel of his twelve-bore into the hole and pulled the trigger.

CHAPTER 9

Second Thoughts

Change, affecting all aspects of life, came to both the farm and village during the fifties and early sixties. In the High Street, the derelict smithy disappeared as builders moved in to erect a new row of council houses, complete with modern conveniences; the ditches running alongside the road were piped and filled in, the grass verges were replaced by kerbstones, and a few widely spaced concrete street lamps were erected. Some thought they were a great improvement, while others complained: 'You can't even see the stars with these bloomin' lights when you go out at night.'

With advancing years and slowing service, Mrs Creek finally had to close her shop in the old bakery, and later a new self-service store which gave Green Shield stamps was built in the field next to the village pond, causing the annual flower show to move into nearby farm buildings and then on to the recreation ground. The second small,

stagnant pond turned even more foul and was filled in, as it was adjudged to have become a hazard to health; similar complaints were made against the cows on the Leys and summer grazing was stopped to placate mothers and newcomers to the village who considered the presence of cow pats in the grass to be both unsightly and unhealthy. The hedge dividing the Leys from the recreation ground was thought to be untidy and was uprooted to make one large grass field, divided only by the exposed footpath.

Developers bought King's Grove, a grass meadow where, as a girl at the village school, Mother had gone each year on Empire Day with the other children, for the annual 'school treat', of games and scrambling for new ha'pennies and pennies. There too in the grove of elms and ashes, Father and his friends had taken young jackdaws, and high up in the trees a rookery gradually grew to raucous life every spring and summer. To the developers, memories of those days of school and birds nesting were unknown; the field had simply been purchased as a site for new houses. The bulldozers and diggers moved in as the young rooks cried greedily for food; the trees were felled, fledglings with broken bones and bleeding bodies were run over by dumper trucks or killed by workman with blows from their spades, and children watched as the field changed. Some were disturbed at the death of the birds and all were shocked when, as the foundations were being dug, a skeleton was found. The police were called in as other ancient bodies were unearthed, until it was decided that in days gone by much more serious games had taken place in King's Grove, for since one of the skulls had obviously been split by a primitive axe, it seemed that the field of Empire Day sports had also been used as a burial ground for soldiers killed in a Saxon battle.

The grove itself did not completely die, as it was preserved in name for the new estate, and the cluster of houses and bungalows that grew up was far more conspicuous than the earlier trees. Unlike the other houses and cottages in the parish they were all very similar to each other and they seemed to stand apart from their surroundings, having little in common with the old village. Finally they were all painted white, which made them look formal and antiseptic, and none of the people who moved in worked in the village, but drove every morning into the town.

An increasing number of villagers joined this morning procession as work with the pen became more respectable, opportunities for employment on the land grew fewer and people gradually deserted the buses and their bicycles for the greater speed and comfort of the car. Bert Nightingale abandoned his bicycle, too, and gradually stopped digging the gardens of others; instead he turned his old wooden garden shed into a shop, filling it with vegetables from his own garden, from those of his neighbours who grew too much for their own consumption and from a visiting greengrocer's lorry. But Bert had neither the head nor the heart for business, seeing all those who came to him not as customers but as friends. Consequently his kettle was always on, his living room had a long succession of visitors with shopping bags and tea cups, and with nearly every purchase each customer was given an orange, a bar of chocolate, or a lettuce, with Bert maintaining that he was merely giving away 'free samples'. With small children he was particularly generous, and those who called for liquorice or dolly mixtures were given almost as much as they bought and nearly all his profit he gave back to those he served. To make matters worse, as his stock gradually increased, with vegetables and tins in his shed, sweets and chocolates in his kitchen, and a jumble of boxes containing anything from toilet rolls to sugar in his spare bedroom, so Bert sampled his own wares throughout the day, sucking sweets and eating chocolates. As he put on weight, his smile grew broader, his girth steadily larger, and his pace considerably slower. His weight affected his legs so much that he stopped gardening altogether, and his sickness benefit had to subsidize his shop and his benevolence.

At the school, three of the old elm trees were felled and an extension was built, turning the Little Room into a store room and providing proper flush toilets. Those who failed the eleven plus went to a secondary school in the next village and were shortly transferred to a brand new *village college*, making those of us at grammar schools envious, for all their facilities and equipment were modern and, while in the spring we had to go on cross country runs, they played football. We travelled to Cambridge to school on an old blue doubledecker bus, with rattling windows and whistling draughts. Each morning and evening it was like a riot on wheels, with caps and satchels flying through the air, accompanied by language so foul that adults riding below were shocked. One afternoon, before the bus had even set out, I was sitting squashed up against a window which proceeded to fall out, thus causing a long delay as we were interrogated by an irate conductor, and during one morning's journey, the behaviour was so bad that the bus was stopped and one boy, who later became a reputable BBC interviewer, was ordered off and had to walk to school. At times, however, the bus became a refuge, for the bus station was the haunt of 'Teddy' boys. The first ones I saw intimidated me by their appearance alone, they were half drunk, drinking from a bottle of sherry, and had greasy hair combed back, knee length coats with velvet collars, bootlace ties, drainpipe trousers, luminous socks, and shoes with thick rubber soles, 'brothel creepers'. In addition they were said to carry cut-throat razors and bicycle chains, and whenever we saw a gang of 'Teds' we kept a respectful distance.

A new vicar arrived at the church, one who appeared to accept high churchmen and non-conformists all as part of the same Christian fold, and so the battle for souls slackened. He was a widower, with a son my age and, for me, playing in the vicarage garden instead of peering through the wall or dancing on the lawn, removed the last of its mysteries. When the vicar suddenly took a new wife, a young woman from his previous parish, the village became alive with tales of his romance;

but as nearly everyone was taken completely by surprise, where all these stories had their origins was never very clear. With some, as always, eyebrows were raised and tongues wagged mischievously, but most wished him well.

The chapel, too, had a new minister, young, pale and fresh out of college, and again he was far different from his predecessor. He had lived in towns all his life and his outlook and theology were quite broad, with fewer restrictions than those emanating from the Welsh valleys and on Saturday afternoons he even played football for the reserve team of the next village. When petrol was rationed during the Suez Crisis in 1956, he taught himself to drive, without help, in a small blue Austin Seven, snaking along the road in fits and starts, and restoring to some their belief in miracles for, somehow, he failed to hit anything. Both he and his wife took some time to adjust to country life; she, used to feeding from tins, served him with uncooked bottled fruit and wondered why he suffered from indigestion and he, on seeing snow on his garden for the first time, telephoned Father to ask if he should sweep it off before it damaged his vegetables.

As we got older, so we were expected, like all good Baptists to take communion, the 'Lord's Supper'. Each person was given a small piece of bread, and then, in individual miniature glasses, 'wine', or more accurately, unfermented grape juice. Several times I asked some of those who viewed with disgust the fact that at the parish church they used real alcoholic wine if Jesus had in fact turned the water in one of his miracles into unfermented grape juice, but I could never get a straight answer. Some chapels, we were told, did not even have grape juice, instead their 'wine' was diluted Ribena; that, it seemed to me, would have been the greatest miracle of all time, if at the wedding feast, Jesus had turned the water into the world's first Ribena. John and Mary were baptised, and baptisms occurred quite regularly. Unfortunately the baptistry developed a leak; in dry weather the water rapidly seeped out, while in wet weather, water originating from the churchyard would trickle in.

It also seemed peculiar to us that each new development, whether television sets, or faster cars, caused some church and chapel-goers to declare that they had to undergo a complete rethink of their beliefs. This I could not understand, nor could I comprehend the reaction of many, including Uncle Jim and Grandmother, to the launching of the world's first satellite, *Sputnik 1* in 1957. That, like television before it, was branded as the work of the Devil and Grandmother asserted that man should not 'meddle in God's firmament'. I wondered if some of them were worried that their departing souls might collide with a Sputnik and so would never get to Heaven, for it seemed illogical to me that if God had made the universe, he would be offended by man exploring his creation.

Others accepted the advance of science as being quite normal, bringing with it no problems of belief or faith. One such man was Great Uncle Bernard who started visiting us quite often when he came to preach at the chapel. He lived in the Fens as a fruit farmer, and each Sunday he would climb into a pulpit, without notes, where he would speak fluently and clearly for as long as was required. But although he was a good preacher, with a phenomenal memory, as soon as he started a service his voice dropped all its regional inflexions and became a sanctimonious monotone, slow, steady, and deep, which, at the Lord's Prayer, always accelerated suddenly, leaving the congregation far behind. Both he and Auntie Mirrie were always welcome as they possessed a dry sense of humour, a deep and lasting belief in God, and they always gave each of us a ten shilling note for pocket money. This generosity was surprising for they had both experienced poverty. Uncle Bernard had worked for others until middle age, when he had started out on his own. The first two years were almost disastrous, with severe late frosts cutting the blossom and leaving the trees almost fruitless, but after surviving two years on the verge of penury, hard work and the good prices of the Second World War came to his rescue and he became comfortably off. His humour and love of the land were reflected in the way he spoke and thought; when out in a cold wind he would say: 'It's a lazy ol' wind boy, it blows right through you', and on seeing the large spades and garden forks that had to be used on our heavy clay he would remark mischievously: 'Ah, the people round here must be strong in the arm and weak in the head'. He was a keen sportsman, often going to Gills Hill for shoots, but there was one sport that he could not abide – fishing. 'Look at all those men', he would mock, 'sitting there drowning worms.'

At chapel we welcomed the reintroduction of carol singing, for it had once been a regular feature of the village Christmas, but had been allowed to lapse. After King's Grove and other new houses had been built, it took two evenings to get round the parish, visiting almost every house. Usually those nights seemed to coincide with sharp frosts, when cars would snake across the corner by the pond, and by the time we arrived at Five Houses the last stop on the first evening, we were usually stamping our feet and rubbing our hands to keep the circulation going. An elderly lady in one of the houses would invite us into her living-room, which was dominated by an old gramophone with a large horn, for tea and biscuits.

It was there, too, that on knocking on the door of Mr Howes, we discovered the truth of one of those early rumours; he really did go to bed early, wearing a long white nightshirt and a matching knitted hat.

In the fields and on the farms other changes were very much in evidence; there were fewer cows, cartloads of manure were being replaced by sacks of artificial fertilizer, cans of insecticide and weed killer became more numerous, and combine harvesters quickly ousted binders from the harvest fields. Father stopped making silage, cutting chaff, and growing mangel-wurzels, hay was baled instead of gathered loosely, and a whole new process of intensive husbandry became essential to improve the crops as prices stayed the same and costs went up. Dividing hedges began to disappear to make larger fields; bigger, better tractors, muck-loaders and spreaders, and larger ploughs meant that fewer men were wanted on the land, battery hens replaced those wandering free, and the whole pace of farming life visibly quickened.

Albert watched these changes cynically. He and his busy, cheerful wife had become our neighbours when they moved into the tied cottage across the road and Albert worked on the farm next to the school. They were both friendly and tolerant, allowing us to retrieve cricket balls from their garden in the summer and to pelt them with snowballs in winter; they both seemed content, too, but in vastly different ways. Mrs Brown showed it in her jovial and sunny disposition, but Albert was only really happy when he felt persecuted and downtrodden; for he was never happier than when grousing, preferably while throwing out thick black mud from the bottom of his ditch which made him feel really under-privileged and added spice to his complaints. His interpretation of history and current affairs always threw new light on old problems; he distrusted all politicians, being convinced that they were all lining their own pockets, he was equally sure that the working man received a bad deal from employers, the Conservative party and the Labour party, yet at the same time his dislike for other groups of highly-paid workers was just as great. He told of how, when he was young and prospects for work on the land had been bleak, he had gone north as a 'Cambridgeshire swede basher', to Normanton in Yorkshire to get better paid work in the mines. His wages had been £3 10s a week, compared with 25s on the farm, and even then, he said, some miners with overtime were drawing £10 each week. As a result, he considered the general strike of 1926, which started in the mines to have been a fiasco; instead of being a great walk-out for better conditions of work and pay as proclaimed by the Labour movement, Albert asserted that the ballot for the strike had been won by young miners who wanted a fortnight off as an extra holiday; when the strike extended beyond a fortnight they were even more content.

The effects of progress came to our farm too, and we greeted enthusiastically our first combine, a small red one, powered by its own engine and towed behind the tractor. Harvest was transformed, the old threshing machines stood uncovered and rotting in the contractors' yards and riding to and fro in the trailer, taking the grain from the field to the barn replaced 'shocking' and carting. The combine did not ease the worry of harvest, however, for although it was faster than the binder, it brought problems of its own, and every day Father finished work tired and covered with dust. The corn had to be cut later than previously, when the individual grains were hard and dry, if it was harvested when not quite fit, it would heat up and turn mouldy and Jim, Father and Charlie would have to shovel tons of it from one bin to another, or even send it away to be dried. As a result harvest became a rush to get in the corn when it was just ripe, for if it was left too late, then other problems would develop; it would shale or, in damp weather, start to germinate in the ear; because of this the habit of Sunday harvest work began to grow, making use of every fine day, but each year our tractors and combine remained silent, hoping that a fine Sunday would extend into the Monday. The straw thrown out in shattered parallel lines across the fields of stubble was baled, with the tractor pulling the baler and its sledge, and the bales were pushed off in heaps of eight or ten to be collected later on trailers.

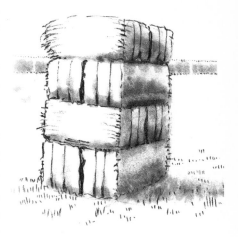

Father also started to grow sugar beet, just a few acres, but that, too, brought more problems. During the summer when other work ought to have been done, it had to be hoed laboriously by hand and in the autumn, as soon as it was due to be harvested, it usually rained, the heavy clay blocked the beet harvester and the individual roots had to be pulled by hand. Each one had to be 'topped' with a beet hook, a job which, with cold hands in a biting wind, was thoroughly unpleasant. The water table fell and an electric motor had to be lowered into the bore hole to push water up into the water tank, and change even came to the cow shed, for ministry officials informed Father that it was unhygienic to milk cows under a thatched roof, so he had to buy and erect a milking bale; an exposed, half open shed, holding four cows at a time, which meant that the milking machines and churns of milk had to be lugged even further each day on an old pair of wheels.

Shortly after the incident with the bull, Percy left the land and, with money in shorter supply, he was replaced by Charlie who worked part-time, as his main job was still in his signal box. Although he came for only a few hours each day, his energy and strength were such that he achieved in an afternoon what most men managed in a day, and his appetite for work never slackened.

161

Coupled with this was an ability to make even the most repetitive job interesting, for, like Jim, he was a keen observer of the local and the national scene and he accompanied his work with a running commentary.

If a certain girl from another village cycled by while he stacked bales of hay or straw he would say; 'There she goes, the village bicycle.'

'The village bicycle?'

'That's right, everybody's ridden her.'

If he heard a cock crow after it had been chasing hens, it would be: 'Listen, 'Cock-a-doodle-do, cock-a-doodle-doo', you know what he's really saying don't you? 'Done 'em all but two, done 'em all but two', and the ol' drake's answering him. 'Quack, quack. Quack, quack. Quite right, quite right'. The sharp-edged call of a great-tit would bring the comment: 'Hark, the ol' saw sharpener's busy today,' for the high-pitched sound was very much like a file being drawn swiftly over hard metal. For everybody and everything, both Charlie and Jim had the most slanderous comments and descriptions to offer, which entertained them through the dullest jobs and the worst weather.

Cousin Diana came to live with us after her father's death on his motorbike, fitting in like another sister and staying until she got married. The old upright telephone with its separate earpiece was changed for something more modern, and jellies and tinned fruit became less like luxuries at the tea table. But other changes came too, far greater than the physical ones in the home and on the land, and ones which threatened to sever our links with the village completely.

After one of Father's brothers died, the butchery business was sold, which meant that, as the farm was part of it, Father would have to buy the farm if he wished to continue farming. This he did, with the aid of a large bank overdraft, which he reduced by selling a thirty-acre field and our old cottage down the road. Consequently, money became scarce and Father's bank statements were always printed in red.

But buying the farm also coincided with another dream that had steadily been growing in his mind, one which would transport the farm, and us, away from the village and place us in Africa; in the

White Highlands of Kenya. There, away from the cold, damp English winters, he saw himself with more land than the 113 acres he had been left with, and while he was improving the land and teaching the natives how to farm, he saw Mother improving the minds of their children by running her own farm school.

Unfortunately, as with so many things, Father's dream broke too late, for Kenya had just experienced four years of terror and bloodshed through the activities of the Mau Mau. (The Mau Mau rebellion started in October 1952 but was virtually over by mid-1956 when the army withdrew from active operations) and already the word 'colonialist' was acquiring a disreputable connotation. The wind of change was beginning to stir the African continent, as well as the corridors of Westminster, and although Father's motives were far divorced from money-making or native exploitation, it was already unfashionable to want to become a 'white settler'. Ignoring the foibles of other people, as usual, and despite the obvious difficulties, he decided to visit Kenya for three months, to find out the facts for himself. Several cows were sold to get some money and to lessen the work for Mother and Jim, and as Jim always refused to deal with the cows, John had to milk each morning before catching the school bus.

From the outset I did not want to leave the farm, but my reason was nothing to do with Mau Mau, wanting to stay in the village, or the thought of leaving my friends; it was solely to do with cricket, which I played obsessively at home and at school, and I was convinced that in Africa I would be able to play hardly at all. My letters to Father during his trip showed my obsession; one, asking initially; 'Have you seen any Mau Mau?' as if they could be found roaming loose in the national parks, immediately went on to describe, for almost the whole of the length of an airmail letter, details of the third day's play of an England *v.* Australia Test Match, and then, more importantly, a ball by ball account of four overs I bowled at school, including derogatory remarks about the fielders each time a run was scored. Diana writing to Father at the same time wrote in a letter: 'Rob hasn't been well, but made a lightening recovery as Games Day got nearer.'

While he was away, Mother managed the farm well, with help from neighbours and relations. Uncle Alfred looked in each day to ensure that there were no problems and Uncle Roy came regularly to cut the lawns with our large and temperamental lawn mower. At times it was almost unmanageable, hurtling across the lawn at top speed, with Uncle trying desperately to control it from behind. Occasionally, to make things more difficult it would burst into flames; when this happened the flames had to be doused with a bucket full of sand, which was always kept in the vicinity, and the machine had to cool while the sand was swept off the grass. Jim and Charlie put in overtime to get all the work done, and George Disbrey also came to help clean out the pigs and cart the hay.

On Father's return it was clear that all doubt in his mind had gone, and he was full of the wonders to be found and seen in Kenya; large fertile farms, the friendliness of the Kikuyu and the Masai, the high altitude and clear air, and the brackish inland lakes, pink with flamingoes. He spent long periods of time talking quietly to Mother, and then they told us that the farm would be sold and that we would definitely be moving. A 'For Sale' notice was put on a field gate, prospective buyers visited; looking, admiring, and criticising, and people in the village began to ask us when we were going to leave. The full implications of emigration gradually dawned on me and went far beyond cricket at school or on the lawn, for I would be leaving the dogs, the cows, the brook, my friends, and home, and I was filled with despondency. It became clear, also that Mother had growing doubts about severing her roots and leaving her family and the village, and an atmosphere tense and uncertain pervaded the house that had once felt so permanent and secure.

One day, a bald headed sculptor and his wife visited, showing little interest in the land, the animals, or the farm buildings, talking only of the house, the enchantment of the thatch and mullion, how this wall could be knocked out to make a studio, and that window enlarged. They seemed to have no deeper feelings for the place, and when I saw them talking enthusiastically to Father, I feared the worst. The man made an offer, a deal was in the offing and Father visited several people for advice; it seemed inevitable that we would go. The final decision came one morning while I was playing cricket on the lawn with Michael, and on going into the house I saw Mother and Father in each others arms by the Aga, crying; the 'For Sale' notice was taken down, the deal was off, and we were to stay.

Father's hopes and dreams had been shattered, and for weeks his eyes and face told of his mental anguish, his disappointment, the lure of Africa and of his memories that still beckoned, but which, for our sakes, he daily ignored. Anticipating selling up, even before his travels, he had been left with few cows, a large overdraft, and had to begin the struggle of survival all over again.

The following years were difficult, with bad harvests, the combine breaking down, there was an outbreak of Johne's disease that caused several cows to fade away and die, making the task of building up the herd even more difficult, and several Saturday mornings, before sending Rachael shopping to the post office and to Bert's, Mother broke down in tears as there was not enough money for all she wanted. For the next few years our summer holidays were spent at home. Mother took up teaching again, and Father seemed to work virtually all the hours of daylight.

In addition, there were still the normal mishaps of farming life; the henhouse roof was blown off and wrapped itself around the greenhouse, the tractor frequently got bogged down in the cloying clay and had to be dug out, and Father's most promising heifer fell down while waiting, tied in the bale, for the inseminator. She broke her neck and died instantly. I too, managed to bring about the death of a porker; it had escaped from its sty one Saturday morning when Father and Mother had gone out, but instead of allowing itself to be driven back, it ran across the main road towards some nearby gardens. I followed in pursuit, over three lawns and through two hedges, until the pig suddenly stopped and slumped to the ground, wheezing far worse than I was. It would not stand again, so I had to carry it back to the farm in a wheelbarrow; no sooner had I returned it to its sty than it rolled over and died. Gradually, however, although the overdraft remained, things improved.

At school my only real interest continued to be sport, causing a number of caustic comments on my report; for French: 'He seems satisfied', for Maths: 'He is not interested', and generally: 'He must take work more seriously,' but for games I got 'Very keen'. During the summer I was preoccupied with cricket and in winter with rugby, often wheezing slowly around the pitch with my head aching and my heart thumping, yet more concerned with putting the ball into the scrum straight than getting a doctor's note excusing me from games.

As 'O' level examinations approached I became somewhat apprehensive, for I did little work, and if I wanted to continue playing cricket at school I would somehow have to pass enough subjects to stay on. As a result I decided to concentrate only on those few subjects in which I stood a remote chance and, unofficially, gave up all those that I knew I would fail. It followed that I was delighted when I was banned from French after the following exchange with the French master:

'What are you eating Page?'

'Nothing, sir.'

'You are eating a sweet boy, I can see that. What have you got in your mouth?'

'Nothing, Sir.'

'For the last time, what have you got in your mouth?'

'Teeth, sir.'

I was made to leave the room, told not to bother with future lessons, and given detention. As I had not been eating anything I felt aggrieved at the prospect of being kept behind after school and approached the master in charge of detention: 'Please sir, my father has gone out for the day and I have got to get home to milk the cows.' I was allowed out, but it was such a bare-faced lie that I suffered from a guilty conscience where none had existed before.

It was at about this time, too, that I lost my temper for the last time. Harvest had just started, and for some reason I became furious with Michael, who was now approaching 6 feet 8 inches in height, and the first weapon that came to hand was a tractor tyre lever of heavy stainless steel. I made as if to throw it, Michael ducked and, while he was still bending down, I really let go, sending it speeding and spinning through the air; it caught him full in the chest and felled him as if dead. John, Father and Mother ran to him, I fled, expecting to hear police tracker dogs at any moment. Returning home at dusk I was surprised and relieved to see Michael with John and two cousins, Ann and Margaret, who almost lived on the farm during holidays. He was still alive, but breathing painfully with a dark bruise over most of his chest. It taught me that the line between sense and savagery is a very narrow one, and that in less fortunate circumstances my behaviour could have been counted as a crime.

Another unusual incident occurred that autumn, and even now is something I cannot explain. One cold clear night, quiet, with a full bright moon, I was woken up by footsteps on the gravel drive. Many times as a small boy I had been frightened by the creaks and groans of the old house during the night and, again, I lay there tense as the footsteps went past my open window. The sound softened as whoever it was walked past the kitchen towards the front garden, perhaps making for the road. I relaxed and tried to get to sleep again, but no sooner had drowsiness returned than the sound of more footsteps brought me back to full consciousness in an instant. The crunching of gravel grew louder, and hardly daring to breathe I climbed out of bed, tip-toed across the room, and peered cautiously out from behind the curtain. There, walking through the gate to the farm was a tramp, clearly visible in the moonlight, with a hat, a beard, an old coat, and our light aluminium ladder over a shoulder. As soon as he was out of sight I hurriedly woke John and then ran to the other end of the house to rouse Father, for I knew he would not want a tramp to be prowling about at night in case a cigarette end was thrown down carelessly near a stack of bales. I got the rifle for my own protection and we all went out to search; the pig sties, the sheds, and around the stacks, but we could find no sign of anyone. Before returning to bed Father went to the front garden as he remembered that the ladder had been left up against an apple tree; it was still there and had obviously not been moved.

As time passed John joined Father on the land, where the steady drone of engines could be heard almost endlessly. Black and white Friesian cows slowly replaced the dairy Shorthorns as they gave more milk and better beef. Battery hens were kept in the old cow shed, which I had to clean out each day for pocket money; only the brook seemed to stay as it was.

CHAPTER 10

All Change

Since those days there has been a continuing process of change throughout the parish. Some of the results have been beneficial, for there is no doubt that the physical burden of the land-worker has been very much reduced and the new tools with which he works has made the struggle against the elements more equal. Jim, now retired, puts it more simply; 'Those who refer to 'the good old days',' he says, 'obviously haven't spent days walking behind a horse and plough in the cold and wet.' But other changes have been as welcome as the death toll that once sounded ominously from the church belfry and, unless harnessed constructively, will kill the village.

The parish of meadows and trees has been transformed and disfig-ured by new developments and modern agricultural techniques, that have, in places, completely destroyed its former beauty and peace. Each year more hedges are grubbed out, trees are felled and, at week-ends, the high pitched whine of chainsaws, belonging to part-time woodmen, competes with the steady hum of the internal combustion engine as weekend motorists drive at a leisurely pace along the roads. The large hedge dividing Tinkers Field in two was uprooted as birds were beginning to incubate, and looking eastwards from the brook, the land has become a treeless tract of gently undu-lating desolation.

Nearly all the fields now come under the plough, the few remaining hedges are trimmed mechani-cally each year, and Father's cows are the last to graze on old-established grass. South of the brook, the once lush meadows are cultivated, the last remnants of the rabbit warren have disappeared, and all that remains of a once fine row of elms is a pile of unburnt tree stumps in the corner. Even the railway beyond has gone and the age of steam and hissing strength has passed into childhood memory. The lines were pulled up, the sleepers removed and in their place a radio telescope now stands; eight reflector dishes strung out in a straight line for three miles, contrasting sharply with their more natural and rustic surroundings and giving a strangely surrealistic quality to the countryside. The scientists say the dishes can pick up radio signals from sources millions of light years away, to probe into the beginnings of time, but Albert, now retired and living in the High Street, sees them differently: 'You don't think they'd spend all that money to look at the stars, do you?' he said to me one morning. 'No, look where they're pointing.' They were all scanning eastwards, Albert presumed in the direction of Moscow.

With the increased use of sprays, even where grass fields remain there is an unusual silence, for on hot summer days the chafing trill of grasshoppers has grown steadily rarer and the roadside verges, trim and neat, are usually silent. Bees often vanish as quickly as they appear after acres of flowering field beans have been dampened by a fine drizzle of spray, and wild flowers wizen and die. In the autumn, wandering along the hedgerows looking for mushrooms is still a pleasure, but on returning home the basket is nearly always empty,

and the only things certain to be found on the land are the machines that dominate it; large self-propelled combines, and the powerful tractors on the larger farms that can pull, with ease, six furrows through the soil.

The aftermath of harvest has taken on a different aspect and there is a new feeling in the air. With the decline of livestock, little straw is needed, and after the combines leave, the fields are fired and the stubble burnt. At dusk the circle of hungry flame grows and a fierce red glow lights the night sky, while on still warm days the sun is shrouded by a pall of mist and smoke which its rays only weakly filter through. Where care is not taken, hedges and trees are lapped by flame, fanned out of control by dry winds, and the scorched branches never again burst into new life. The fields wait charred and black for the ploughman, relieved only by the spotless white undersides of lapwings as they take to the air in sudden and erratic flight.

Not only has the look of the land changed, but so, too, has its value. At the end of the war it could be purchased for £40 per acre, but now even acres of thick clay can fetch up to £1,000. As a result, those farming families who wish to retain their links with the land are faced with death duties and capital gains which make their situation extremely tenuous. It seems likely that many will be forced off the land because of these economic pressures, and a once traditional occupation will become the property of trust fund managers and wealthy businessmen wanting a hobby as well as an investment. Some may argue that in such circumstances the farmer should cash in and sell up, but most, like Father, are working farmers, not land speculators; to them the value of their land is measured by the sweat they have spilled over it, the paper value is meaningless, and, if they want to keep farming, worthless too.

In the winter of 1962–63 a transformation came to the country-side quite unrelated to the activities of man, for frost held land and water in its shivering grip, freezing the brook and pond, and turning the fields cold and solid. Snow fell and lingered, icicles clung to the wire over the thatch, and everywhere was crisp, white and glowing. Weeks turned into months; each morning Father had to lag the frozen water taps with hot rags and the land became too hard to plough. The intense cold drove a smallholder from his four acres, with its hens and geese, and foxes preyed on the fowl; as his hunger increased and his companions diminished an old gander strode along the road and into the farmyard where he has stayed ever since. When spring finally came and the ice slowly melted and the snow turned to slush, normality did not return, for friendly but thieving

magpies were absent from the trees and fields, the laughing call of green woodpeckers was missing, kestrels and sparrow hawks had disappeared, tawny and little owls no longer interrupted the night, and along the brook, kingfishers were never seen and the barn owls had vanished with the snow.

Some said the cold had killed them, others that sprays and pesticides had weakened their resistance, and finally led to their destruction; all we knew was that once familiar birds could be seen no more. Since then, some have reappeared; tawny owls can once again be heard at night, but little owls are seldom seen and barn owls never. Kestrels once more hover for food, patient and pitiless, but the ferocious sparrowhawks are still absent. Kingfishers returned to the brook after an absence of eight years but magpies are still uncommon, and recently I thought I heard a woodpecker; I looked up hopefully, but all I saw was a starling, mimicking, but at least it had heard a woodpecker somewhere, and perhaps they too will soon be back.

The return of the kestrels was particularly pleasing as they had always been common and their disappearance was a real loss. Now they are back and breeding, for two years ago I found a young bird flapping helplessly on the bank of the old railway bridge, with a broken wing, as if hit by a passing car. Its curved, cruel bill, drew blood from my hand easily, and its talons were like needles; its features formed a unity of frightening beauty, and looking into its deep brown eyes was like looking backwards in time, almost to creation. With Father's help and some sticking plaster from Dr Simpson, the injured wing was set; covered with sticky brown paper which was then held in place by the plaster. It soon became quite tame, perching on my arm and seeing me as a supplier of food, usually sparrows, which for the first time in many years made me pick up a rifle. Each dead sparrow was seized by a talon and then, after sometimes plucking the breasts and wings with its beak, it would begin to eat, starting at the head, penetrating the skull as easily as an egg shell, and working downwards. When the plaster was removed, and the paper soaked in water was peeled off, the wing had healed. But on this occasion we were determined not to make the same mistake as with the owl and decided to keep it until strength had completely returned and it could kill live mice.

I then changed my mind, for an old friend from the next village had always wanted a bird of prey to train with leash and lure for fal-

conry, but he had never been successful. Once he had kept a kestrel, which was then stolen from his garden, so I gave him the bird, hoping that with time he could forge the delicate link between falcon and falconer. Rufus thrived in his care, living on live mice and locusts, until one February day, with the sun unusually warm after an icy night, the door of the shed was opened at feeding time, and the kestrel flew out. It perched on the roof of the house for several minutes and then flew back into the wild. What happened with freedom remains a mystery; perhaps rheumatism set into the fused bone and the bird slowly died, as Socrates the owl had done. I like to think that it lived on into the summer, to take food to a brood of three or four fluffy young in a hole at the top of a high elm.

After myxomatosis small colonies of rabbits re-established themselves, not in warrens, but in dense hedges and along ditches, to suffer every three or four years from a fresh cycle of disease; they survived the cold, however, scraping snow from the grass, and so did the foxes, and their numbers have increased ever since. Their visits to the farm have also become more numerous and one morning I was woken at first light by the latest labrador, Tinker, barking and straining on her chain. On looking out of my bedroom window I could see the reason, for a fox sat just ten yards away from her, watching quizzically as the bitch nearly choked herself with rage. I was up early on another morning too, to see if there were cubs at the Warners Corner earth. After several minutes watching and seeing nothing I walked over to the entrance, and as I peered in, a cub, only about a month old, peered out. The sun was rising behind me, and as I stood motionless, with branches of an elder bush on either side, the cub did not notice. It came out, followed by two others; playful, alert, and full of life, just like puppies, running to within a yard of my feet. My arms and legs soon ached, and at the first slight movement they vanished underground and did not reappear.

Indeed my fascination for foxes since having Cassius has continued, and even now I have a vixen, too tame to leave the farm, but too wild to release. She has escaped twice but returned on both occasions; the first time she was away for over a day and returned at night. She squealed when I called her name, and approached me with wagging brush. The second time her freedom lasted only a minute; she escaped when Rachael opened the door to feed her, but on seeing a hen she ran at it, seized it and immediately dragged it back to her shed. Several months earlier I had been given a small cub, named Sidney, that had been dug from an earth to be killed, and I hoped that in due course the two would breed, although it is said that foxes

174

seldom mate in captivity. Whereas the vixen is quite small, Sidney grew into a fine dog fox; alert, greedy, and playful, with a large brush and a soft thick coat. Unlike Cassius, he enjoyed water, and everything that moved he chased, including bumble bees; those he caught in his mouth he chewed and swallowed with obvious enjoyment. The experiment did not take place, however, for as the breeding season approached, Sidney escaped and did not return.

Despite my affection for foxes, and Father's tolerance, they do much damage; one morning we found a dozen hens killed for no reason, and neighbours have lost even more. In fact, a year ago, their visits became so regular and the bitch's anger became so great, that several nights I had to get up and let her off her chain, and once I picked out three pairs of eyes reflecting back the beam of my lantern. After one outburst of barking I let Tinker off her chain and she trapped a full grown fox beneath a slightly raised hen house, which was just high enough to allow a fox to crawl under, but just low enough to keep a dog at bay. I got the rifle from the house and decided reluctantly that I had to shoot it. I lay on the ground in my pyjamas with the fox completely exposed in torchlight, and its head

lined up in the sights. Just as I was going to pull the trigger it moved, and I noticed that it was wearing a collar; it was Sidney. I could not shoot, called the dog away, and let him go. After that, Father set a snare, but only succeeded in catching a cow when they all got out one night, and the foxes were only frightened off when we allowed the dog to wander free at night.

But the greatest change of all in the parish has come to the brook; suddenly and dramatically when the River Authority decided to 'clean it out'. Mechanical scoops and bulldozers arrived to gouge out the bed and clear the banks; as a result the murmuring shallows and quiet pools, the pike and perch, and the meandering wildness have virtually all disappeared. Many of the trees along the banks were felled, the water lilies and reedmace have been replaced by calculations of depth and flow and, much to the satisfaction of the engineers who planned the transformation, it has become a shallow and uniform drainage channel. Its banks are now covered with thistles and teasels, the fish have nearly all died, and the Jungle, obscured beneath spoil, is only just recovering as wilderness. The men scooping out mud, scooped out with it a 5 pound tench, eels which they put in sacks to take home to fry, and a 15 pound pike; those pike left behind quickly became emaciated and sickly, and as the water level fell and their food disappeared, they died and floated away, bellies upwards. Now the brook is little more than a ditch, as barren and plain as a drainage expert's drawing board; in summer it fills up with green slime and spirogyra; the sheep wash has been filled in, the otters' tree has been uprooted, the pond has dried up, the frogs and dragonflies have disappeared, and the sun has set for the last time in torrents of reflected light on water. But, we are told, we should be pleased with what has happened, 'for the brook will flood no more.'

In many ways, life on the farm remains very much the same as it has always been. At times it is still hard; during one harvest the land became so wet that the combine got bogged down and water squelched in the wheelings. Even the large machine of the Gills Hill uncles could not get all the grain, and that in the bins heated up, while that still out in the fields rotted. Misfortune is still a regular occurrence, with difficult calvings and a cow catching a teat on some barbed wire, and bleeding to death. But at other times, it is still

pleasant, at bale cart under a June sun or riding on the back of the
drill on a spring day, with an occasional migrating white-rumped
wheatear inspecting the disturbed soil, and large flocks of golden
plovers, whistling plaintively, settling on the fields of winter wheat.
Much of the work has become easier, the cattle food is mixed with an
electric mixer, concrete has replaced mud in the farmyard, the pigs
have gone, with calves now occupying the vacated pig sties, the hens
are again in deep litter, a self-propelled combine awaits harvest for
the first time, and the milking bale now holds eight cows. The milking process has completely changed, with the bale enclosed and the
milking machines drawing milk from the udders and sucking it along
a pipe line into a refrigerated tank of stainless steel; every morning,
instead of the daily heaving of churns, a tanker lorry attaches a tube
to the milk tank, and sucks the milk away. Father's liking for cows
remains, and we, as well as Charlie, still eat 'bisnings', although officially it is described as being unfit for human consumption. He also
continues to have a number of bright ideas; his most recent was to
lessen the distance he has to walk for the cows each year. Now the
cows have Plaid, a young border collie, forever yapping at their heels,
a brave and self-willed dog, who, when he gets a flying hoof in the
face, becomes even wilder and more determined. When, and if, his
eagerness slows he will be a most useful dog, unless, like many country dogs, he wanders on to the roads where cars are driven fast
through the village, and the authorities will not allow a speed limit;
'Oh no, you can't have a speed limit, your accident-injury rate is not
high enough, and you have had no fatalities. If the situation changes
let us know'.

With the decrease in mud for nests, swallows build less frequently
in the sheds and hen houses, preferring it seems, to nest in trees nearer the brook. The gander remains and now has a mate, but sadly he
also has rheumatism, and just at the vital moment when new life
could be created, his leg gives way, which means that the goose eggs
are always infertile. Although Jim no longer accompanies him,
Charlie still works with amazing energy and strength, but his movements have slowed with age and the development of a limp. Yet,
despite the fact that Dr Simpson continues to practice as a genuine
family doctor, Charlie is reluctant to go to him. 'What can he do?' he

says, 'my father limped as he got older, so I will too.' Sometimes he swings his leg so much, that Bert at the post office describes him as 'the only person to limp while riding a bike.'

Great Uncle Bernard also visits the farm regularly, after moving into the cottage along the road from which George Disbrey moved into a new old people's bungalow. There he has transformed the garden into a piece of replica fen, removing most of the trees and bushes and planting every available piece of soil with vegetables and soft fruit. One Sunday morning before the last of the pigs went to market Father put the boar in with a sow: 'How disgraceful, putting them in together on a Sunday!' I said to Uncle, seeing him in his best suit. 'Ah well, you know what they say boy. Better the day, better the deed.' Even now he preaches regularly without notes, and is known to everybody as Uncle.

Each summer, as always, the atmosphere in the farmhouse seems thick with country smells, jam, marmalade, chutney or horseradish being made, but blackberries, plums and beans are now put into plastic bags and deep-frozen instead of bottled or salted. Father knocked out the living room grate to reveal a large open fireplace and an old faggot oven in the wall, and when cold east winds blow the house still fills with smoke. Wrens, robins, thrushes and blackbirds, continue to provide a dawn chorus of song in the garden, and sparrows nest in the roof, where thatchers will again soon be working.

The main road just past the farm has been widened and there is talk of a six-lane motorway being sited just north of the village. Most people think it is odd that the planners should take up a railway, and then have to plan a motorway for the resulting heavy lorries. It is even odder that in addition, the motorway will interfere with the radio telescope, for which planning permission was also given, and it seems indicative of the way in which planners think that the telescope looks millions of light years backwards.

For the village and those who work in it, the passage of time has brought considerable alteration and disruption; the old village roadman had gone, as has the policeman on his bicycle, the rag and bone man no longer calls for custom, and Chronicle died peacefully in his bed. In their places, a large yellow lorry sweeps the road, a Panda car represents the Law, rags and bones are put into black plastic bags with the rest of the rubbish for the refuse men, who no longer have to carry dustbins, and who or what will clean out the council ditches is unknown. Bert Nightingale's shop is no more and his smile and free samples are missed by the children who once bought his sweets. With decimalisation, business became even harder for Bert, and he continued to deal in pounds, shillings and pence; those who wanted to use the new currency usually had to do their own conversion and Bert would hand them one of numerous tins of money so that they could take out their own change. When his heart finally gave out, the village mourned; it needn't have, for Bert was not happy with the growing complications of modern life and, for good measure, he was spared from the mysteries of Value Added Tax.

As the old characters slowly fade away, new ones do not appear, and strangers with large cars or money for modernisation buy up their houses as the commuters of suburbia consider the village to be a desirable place in which to live. The old villagers often look on the newcomers with suspicion, even hostility, while the newcomers regard those with rustic accents and manners as being semi-literate country bumpkins. But the changes and difficulties are much greater than this simple confrontation suggests, for the price of property is causing a change in the actual structure of the village. Bert's old house, with three small bedrooms, damp walls, an overgrown garden, and a bucket lavatory fetched £11,250. Other expensive estates have followed King's Grove, most fitting in quite well, but one standing out from its surroundings, built with a brick and design usually reserved for public conveniences. Most of these estates are dormitories, empty during the day and dead at night; the residents usually stay for a year or two, and then with a change of job or promotion, the 'For Sale' notices appear and they move away. They are rather like sophisticated gypsies, with the pantechnicon replacing the coloured hand-painted vardo – the old horse-drawn gypsy caravan – and a succession of new housing estates forming the camp sites. The length of stay does not allow adults or children to put down roots and the houses become a refuge in which material possessions are of prime importance, neighbourliness of no account, and reality is shut outside.

In the past, as cottages became vacant, they were bought or rented by young village couples wanting to start out on their own, but now such properties are becoming beyond local pockets, and villagers wanting a house have to look for council accommodation in the towns, or wait and hope with 'in-laws' until a place becomes vacant nearer home. Even when that happens, many are earning too much to get a council house and not enough for a mortgage, and so the newcomers also bring with them a new wealth that is changing the village community from a mixture of classes and backgrounds, to a one-class residential area, and that class is upper middle.

Gardens, if they have not been sold off for yet another building plot, blaze like pages from a colour brochure, with all the daisies removed from the lawns and trees of flowering cherry neatly pruned. Old patches of brambles, cow parsley, and nettles are cut down for tidiness, and even the pink flowering soapwort on the Leys, once used by country people in the manufacture of soap, was sprayed as a weed. The hedges and scrub at each end of the Leys have been replaced by smart fences and, at any sign of 'wild' behaviour, complaints are sent to the parish council. Mr Holben's old house is hemmed in by new buildings, on one side 'superior designed houses', and on the other a large and expensive bungalow that would have been more appropriate on the high veldt.

With effluent surreptitiously allowed to flow from septic tanks into the ditches, the pond has turned murky and watercress is seldom found. Each evening, the White Horse is bathed in white light and inside beer, skittles, darts, a one-armed bandit and a juke box bring in the trade. Even the chapel has changed, with padded chairs replacing the hard wooden benches and central heating giving a uniform warmth. Strict Sabbath observance has almost disappeared and every Sunday morning, worshippers with wash leathers and plastic buckets bow down before the new chromium plated Gods, from Fords and General Motors. Old people living alone have 'meals on wheels', and if they become too much trouble they are sent away by busy relatives.

The old bakery has been knocked down and a row of old people's bungalows erected, while at the school, nearly a hundred children attend and play in an enlarged playground, where the last of the old elms has been felled. In many ways, the children have suffered from change more than any other group; the facilities provided for them are good, but as soon as it snows, salt is sprinkled on icy roads and gardens are looked on by many parents as show pieces, rather than places where their children can play, and everywhere they are faced by petty restrictions, regimentation, and conformity.

But, fortunately, some of the spirit of the old village survives; the football team has been revived and on Saturday afternoons a unique rustic version of soccer is played out against neighbouring villages on the recreation ground and, with a tablet from the doctor, I too can play without a wheeze. Shorts are now shorter, boots are lighter and the ball is now covered with a light coat of water proofing vinyl and no longer gets heavier as the match progresses; but although the ball and football fashions have changed, village rivalries have been passed down from one generation to the next. The village flower show brings villagers and newcomers together, as does the Horticultural Society, the Bowls Club, the Men's Club and the Women's Institute, and efforts are made to retain the feeling of a community. There are also welcome flashes which show that independence of thought and deed are still abroad in the parish. The President of the Women's Institute, who works hard for the village, has little in common with the normal buxom, flowery hatted caricature of these ladies, with large houses and big ideas; she is the wife of Pegger's 'Man Jackson', living in a still unmodernised council house, riding an ancient bicycle, and her accent only becomes refined when she is in the chair at a meeting, or uses the telephone. At dusk, the crash of twelve-bore cartridges can sometimes be heard where no guns ought to be. Old Mrs Hawkes still cooks and lights her small thatched cottage by paraffin, not wanting to be connected up to the electricity supply. And recently, when mains sewerage came to the village for the first time, she did not want a flush toilet built in her house. Instead, against all well-meaning advice, she had it constructed in a small asbestos shed at the bottom of her garden, where the old bucket lavatory had stood. Albert continues to look on 'civilisation' with complete cynicism, and occasionally a girl on a horse rides into the middle of the main road to run at, and jump, the Leys fence, and gallop across the grass, almost defiantly.

Defiance is also to be found at meetings of the Parish Council, where battles are fought with planners, plotters and office-bound bureaucrats. Matters relating to street lamps and refuse collections are discussed with urgency and sometimes anger, and letters are sent to men in high places complaining about stubble fires, heavy lorries and inefficiency, in the hope that misplaced progress can be checked and the identity and the character of the village retained.

Often, other vital issues are discussed, such as whether smoking should be allowed at council meetings. Recently, Tom Murkin, an unrepentant smoker, was confronted by Ruby, my childhood aunt, and now receptionist at the doctor's, and an arch opponent of the tobacco 'drug'.

'The trouble with you Tom Murkin,' she exclaimed, 'is you can't think straight as your mind's all smoke.'

'And the trouble with you Ruby,' came the immediate reply, 'is you're all wind.'

Tom had an answer, too, when the clerk read out a letter from a government department wanting to know the last known addresses of some deceased trustees of the village institute. 'That's easy,' he said, 'tell 'em the Churchyard.'

The same subject came up at the Annual Parish Meeting: 'What do they want to know that for?' somebody asked.

'They want to write to them of course,' came the automatic response.

Many scoff at parish pump politics, but at least in village affairs all villagers have an opportunity to air their views and grievances, which is certainly not the case at more grandiose institutions of democracy.

In some respects, the village is fortunate, for although it is changing, it has not yet suffered as some of its neighbours. Two villages nearby have been swamped by large estates that have completely overrun and obscured the original settlements, and village life as it was known has been lost for ever. Others have experienced the exact reverse, with no development being allowed, meaning that the villages have almost completely run down; at one, no new houses have been built for young couples, the population has become aged, the village school has been closed, the shop and pub see little custom, and there is a strange feeling of decay in the air.

How long my own village will retain its individuality is hard to foresee, although it is obvious that the whole structure is changing and the old country values and way of life are rapidly disappearing. This can not be attributed to progress alone, for blame must also be apportioned to individuals who lack a certain care and concern for their environment; to those who have systematically planned the destruction of a community and a countryside, to some farmers who regard their land solely in terms of profit, to owners and builders who only see gardens and fields as potential high density building plots, and to those who fail to recognise the importance of family and community life, and who are forever assuming that the grass will always be greener after the next move and beyond the next overdraft.

Perhaps there will be new generations to give life and spirit to the village; children feeling the free wind on their cheeks as they roam

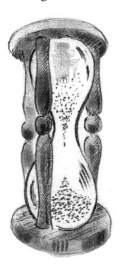

the open fields; old men exchanging tales and memories in the High Street; cows slowing the traffic along the roads as they return each day to the farm for milking, and larks climbing high in the sky to greet the summer sun with a tribute of early morning song. Or, more likely, the unremitting march of the prairie farmers, the decline in neighbourliness, the container lorries growling along the roads, and the churning of cement mixers, will continue unabated and should be seen as an obituary notice, already in preparation, for the death of another English village. Only time will provide an answer.

Thirty Years On

———

To those old preachers in the chapel pulpit, thirty years was nearly half a lifetime – but it has gone – surreptitiously, quickly; where has it gone? An old lady of 95, just taken to her bed for possibly the last time, has summed up the passage of time, the passing of life: 'When I was a small child a day seemed like a lifetime – now it seems to be Christmas every day.'

Thirty years have gone, disappeared, and in that time the heart of the village has died, with its soul hanging on, but only just. In that time I have written thousands – maybe millions of words about the countryside, the wildlife and the people I love – but it has made no difference; the pen mightier that the sword? I don't think so. The pen mightier than the chainsaw, the plough, the bulldozer, the cement mixer, the planner, the politician, the ill-considered regulation, the European Directive? I don't think so.

They have been thirty years of laughter and tears – hope and dis-appointment – but above all they have been thirty years of political betrayal, in which village life, country life, have taken second place and third place to the superficial Gods of 'progress', 'efficiency' and 'development'.

In that time, the old people of the farm and village have gone – Ruby, Albert, Uncle, Charlie, Jim, Bert the postman and Jack Hawkes, the 'Daddy Long Legs' of the old village football team. My Mother and Father have gone too – their departure marked with tears, memories and thanks. I had a full two years of tears when those closest to me, family and friends decided to die, or at least somebody decided for them.

So great was the need that I even bought a new pair of shiny, black, leather shoes – my 'funeral' shoes.

My Father's death left me numb. Admitted into Addenbrooke's Hospital, the 'world famous' teaching hospital in Cambridge, he was discharged two days later – diagnosis 'constipation'. One week later he died, just off the operating table – diagnosis under the knife, 'bowel cancer'. We watched his life slowly fade away; tears fell in abundance as they do now as I write. It is an honour and a privilege to regard your Father as a friend: there is no honour in dying without

dignity with your tongue strapped to your lower jaw. In an age of litigation we took no action. Hospital money should be for patients, not lawyers – but perhaps young doctors ought to be taught the difference between Syrup of Figs and the need for a scalpel.

We buried him on a mild morning in early autumn. From the church to the farm he rode in comfort – from the farm to his burial field he rode in style. Two fine Shire horses with polished leather and brasses pulled a trailer on which his coffin rested – laying on that was just one solitary wreath made from the wild hedgerow harvest. What emotion: the funeral master walking slowly ahead, with top hat in place; the long-lost sound of heavy horses, with those following behind, on foot, stopping the traffic. He chose the spot, by a hedge in the brook meadows, my Mother's ashes at his feet. I had asked to see him in his coffin to make sure the hospital had got the body right – it had – miraculous – but better right in life than death.

As handfuls of soil showered into the hole, sprinkled by those who were so moved, it really was dust to dust, ashes to ashes: it was more – it was soil to soil. He was in the element that had grown him wheat and grass and had helped him produce grain and milk. A farmer's wealth is his soil and into it he took his memories, his experience, his wisdom, his country lore and weather lore. With him too went honesty, decency, his love of his rural culture and his part in his community. Gone – soon he would be part of the spring, re-growth, new harvests and lark song high in this wide lowland sky. 'Robin', the

185

vicar said with his voice trembling, 'this has been unusual for me – a funeral with real meaning.' It was – and on that day I booked my funeral spot in a hedge in the brook meadow – next to Bramble, my little lurcher – my numbness had gone.

In thirty years, the old farmers and the old farms have gone. Farming itself has changed almost beyond recognition too – thanks to a political and bureaucratic abomination called the Common Agriculture Policy – CAP. In 1973 the British people were duped into joining something called the European Economic Community – an area, so we were told, for free trade. The long-term aim of course was no such thing – it was a 'European Union' involving political, economic and social integration – a European Superstate. As the Berlin Wall and the tyranny of the Soviet Union's Eastern European Superstate crumbled – a number of unscrupulous British politicians were quite knowingly weaving us into a Western European Empire, not much different from the crumbling Eastern model based on elitism, central control, deception and the democracy of the ant hill – in other words no democracy at all. Of course, those wanting to put their snouts in the political and financial troughs were enthusiastic – to them black was white, right was wrong and democracy was whatever would give them power and bring the brimming troughs into their sad, one-dimensional lives.

Brussels sprouts

Every week Brussels issues over 100 new rules that we MUST obey.

REFERENDUM PARTY
its now or never – let the people decide

As part of the deception, the pound too was set to disappear – lost to the 'Euro'. It was then that the multi-millionaire Sir James Goldsmith, father of Zac, became involved – 'to save the pound'. His view was simple; 'lose your currency – lose your sovereignty'. The mainstream politicians, fearing his influence and his money, promised a Referendum on the currency – as a result, amazingly, Britain still has the pound and the popular mood has swung against the 'Euro' of political deception.

During the election of 1997 'Sir Jimmy' flew into the Warner's Corner field by helicopter to meet villagers at The Hoops. Later in the year, tragically, I polished my funeral shoes for him too.

Farming and fishing were the traditional ways of life to suffer most under the EEC/EU/the United States of Europe. Most countries value their 'primary producers' – not Britain. The bulk of our valuable fishing grounds were given away to become a 'European resource', leaving our fishing communities devastated. Farming, too, ceased to be a way of life involving real people, in a living and working countryside, the bureaucrats saw it simply as a means of food production which must be made more efficient, more competitive; 'agri-business' must replace 'agriculture' – welcome to the CAP. Welcome to the CAP – and goodbye to our beautiful herd of dairy cows – black and white British Friesians. 'Britain has a milk lake and a butter mountain' *they* told us. *They* lied as usual; it was Germany and France that had created a European milk lake and butter mountain through over production, and Britain's dairy farmers had to help

reduce the surplus by killing their cows – thousands of cows – hundred of thousands of good, healthy cows, as a condition for entry into the EEC. From dairy self-sufficiency, Britain became an 80% producer, importing the balance from the European milk lake and butter mountain.

It was not sold to the public as a cynical buy-out, a mass cow murder for a centralised system of production control – the truth was hidden in the jargon of the bureaucrat and the lying politician with phrases and words such as 'the rationalisation of production' – 'the stability of the market place' – 'subsidy', 'quota', and a 'brighter future for British farmers'. Three hundred thousand British dairy cows were bought for slaughter – they had no future – black or white – bleak not bright – the farmers were told 'cash today' will yield gold tomorrow. I could not watch without tears, as the lorries loaded up in the farmyard; horses yesterday, cows today and farmers tomorrow?

Since then the ploughshare and chemical spray have ruled supreme, aided and abetted by Dutch Elm Disease. The fungus arrived in the bark of imported elms – imported illegally with their bark still attached and overlooked by idle officials not doing their jobs. The effect has been deep and devastating. In a landscape dominated by the elm for hundreds of years, the elm has virtually gone, the most majestic of trees has almost disappeared. What the prairie farmers started, Dutch Elm Disease finished. Thirty years ago, I could not imagine the village without elms, those fine old hedgerow trees with their grooved bark and the sound of summer breezes in their leaves. A rookery appeared in the trees of the spinney a few years before their end and the calls of the birds became a reassuring part of everyday life. Then the disease came.

The spread was slow and unremitting. We hoped and prayed that it would miss us, then the first tell-tale signs arrived: leaves brown as if scorched by fire, or cut by frost – in full summer. Over four or five years all the trees fell victim and most were cut down. The landscape opened out and distant street lights could be seen shining at night where no signs of settlement had been seen before.

The tree where I saw my first kestrel chicks died. The ancient trunk where I found the fox cubs blew over and the rooks found they had to search for other places to nest. Now no jackdaws breed

188

in the southern half of the village – there are simply no large trees with accommodating holes – and the rooks have dispersed over the whole parish – a few in the willow trees by the brook; a few more in the tall trees of Holben's old house and a small cluster in the vicarage garden.

I miss the elms, the haze of a fresh green spring, the cool shade at harvest's edge and the golden yellows of autumn days. They were

friendly, reassuring trees; they had always been there; they linked present with past and past with future. Through folly their reign was broken and the elms died.

Our fourteen farmyard swallows' nests of childhood disappeared, as did the corn bunting, the English partridge, the song thrush, the once common brown hare, and has anybody heard a cuckoo? Even the once teeming house sparrow has become scarce. We kept our hedges, our grass and some beef cows – but one bright summer day I was puzzled – something was missing – a familiar part of my landscape – my skyscape – was gone. What was it? I looked – I listened – I worried – I thought – and then it came to me – shocking me – hurting me – I could not hear a lark: the summer song of the skylark had been silenced – the anthem of an English summer taken away.

Wildlife has not been the only part of the parish and its immediate surroundings to disappear, in just thirty years, six farms have vanished – absorbed by larger holdings with some of the fields ploughed by a twelve furrow plough. The farmyard where my Mother spent her childhood in the High Street has been turned into executive houses and each year young 'suits' called Rupert or Julian, knock on my door and say; 'Your farmyard is in the 'village envelope' you know – we could help you to develop it.' They make smooth sounding sentences and mention sums of money with many noughts, conjuring up visions of 'Bird's Farm Pastures', a cul-de-sac of executive houses – leading the imagination to white beaches, cricket in Barbados and a life of luxury – there is only one snag – I want my farmyard to remain a farmyard.

In thirty years, the trickle from the land has become a torrent with hundreds of thousands of farmers and farmworkers joining the exodus and as I write there is a farming suicide every six days. The promised gold of the CAP became fools' gold covered with misery and disillusion. Even my brother joined the ranks of 'ex-farmers' – preferring the life of a college porter to the insecurity of the land. So I have become a farmer in my own right – with the farm subsidised by the pen. The unknowing complain of 'farm subsidies' – yet cheap food is a subsidy received by every household in the country, paid for by those still working on the land who fail to get a fair reward for their labour and their produce.

The village itself has changed too. 'Mobility of labour' still rules – with people coming and going, and rarely staying any length of time. *Mobility of labour?* Why not *stability of labour?* Encouraging just that, *stability* – with its roots, social cohesion, continuity, culture and community. Roots? What are they? What part of the town planning syllabus were they in? Rural culture – what is it? – I haven't had time to notice.

Of those who attended the village school with me, just four remain, with two living in their old family houses. The rest have been forced out, unable to afford the prices. My own semi-detached ex-farmworker's cottage is worth £250,000: an absurdity beyond my comprehension. To me, it is worth nothing, as I want to continue living in it: it is home, not a fleeting investment opportunity.

Others see things differently; the Diocese of Ely has sold the Vicarage, in the heart of the village's conservation area. There stands the church, the pub, the post office, the village school and the old Burwash Manor Farm. The vicarage has been bought and 'restored' by a wealthy property developer; the nearby church bells have been 'muffled' and the 'vicar' is now a lady in a dog collar with three parishes to maintain, living in the next village. Old Miss Webb – with her eggs and black dress, left her fields to the church to help maintain the stipend of the vicar; her wishes seem to have been forgotten. It would appear too that the church Establishment had a choice between God and Mammon. Mammon has apparently won.

The Squire's old house has also changed, turned into offices. More astonishingly, the tiny thatched cottage where Mrs Hawkes was the last villager to cook on a paraffin stove has been 'modernised' and turned into two 'starter homes' at £145,000 each. Changing direction in the kitchen is by three-point turn.

Worse is to come: urban politicians – rootless and ruthless – have promised thousands of new houses for the area that could swamp and surround the parish. Indeed, as I write, a plan for a thousand new homes has apppeared for land close to the village. If they come there will be yet more commuters; more high-tech industries of uncertain duration – designed and permitted to create short-term phoney growth. Phoney growth? Yes, phoney – just as in the Industrial Revolution, the housing development of the High-Tech Revolution is about moving sections of the population from one part of the country to another, for economic convenience. From the cramped terraces of the old coal and iron towns to the tarted-up little boxes of 'Sunny Meadows Development', it is clear that the planners and economists have learnt nothing.

Ignoring the possible deluge of immigrants as the boundaries of the European Union move east, the natural predicted population growth of Britain is just 0.18% per year. Hardly justification for the proposed planning illiteracy. Perhaps the politicians could try moving jobs to people, rather than people to jobs – the *saved community* rather than the *free market*.

The village school remains in the centre of the village – with the children joined by those from the neighbouring village of Grantchester. But few children now play in the fields or could name the flowers that grow in the roadside verges, or the birds that sing in the quieter dawn chorus. Many of them have become detached from nature. Just as many incoming parents live suburban lives – so their children live 'in the country' but they are no longer 'of the country'. Despite numerous attempts to ban hunting, the Trinity Foot Beagles can still be heard baying for food at feeding time. Somehow urban politicians driven by egos and political correctness consider the chasing of a few hares and foxes as being more outrageous than battery hens, collie dogs kept in London flats and the increased pollution from 'globalisation'.

The visits of some individuals to the village are very brief. Shortly before Christmas one year – didecoys – the local name for 'travellers', spilled out of a van, felled a holly tree in the churchyard, cut it up and were off again inside five minutes, with their stolen Christmas decorations. One of the ancient village water pumps was unscrewed and taken away, no doubt to be sold to a garden centre; and shortly after the death of my father, the farmhouse was burgled. The post office was raided by nice men wearing balaclavas and wielding iron bars, and the farmyard is regularly visited by uninvited guests at night. As a result, I can no longer keep diesel for the tractors on the farm as it gets stolen and the village policeman has gone; after every theft the police rarely call – they seem more concerned with political correctness and parking fines than fighting the escalating rate of rural crime.

After one theft of diesel I phoned the police. 'I expect the didecoys did it,' I said in exasperation. 'We don't call them didecoys any more Sir', came the pompous reply. 'Well we do', I answered him, 'and we still call you coppers.' Sadly that was only a half truth – the usual phrase is 'useless bloody coppers'.

Just north of the village disaster struck in the late 'seventies with the construction of a motorway. The M11 is an intrusion – giving pollution of noise, light and air. The 'street architecture' of lamp-posts, roundabouts and feeder roads are all urban in a rural setting – colleges of further education evidently supply courses in 'town planning' not 'rural planning'. Where I once watched badgers in silence and moonlight, there is now nothing but the roar of traffic and the glare of lights. It was 'sold' to the locals as 'The Cambridge Western By-pass'. The reality was far different. Years ago 'Daddy Long Legs' was shown a plan indicating a key motorway linking the Midlands with London; so allowing Stansted to become a major 'London Airport'. The 'By-Pass' was a part of a whole – deception again? Of course. Now as I walk in the brook meadows at dusk, to check my sheep – there in the southern evening sky I count lights – not stars – moving lights, planes at Stansted – eight, ten, twelve. Soon, we are promised, another runway; the protesters of course will lose as the planning system is weighted against them – and democracy.

Fortunately all is not lost, for there are still signs of hope. Although diminished there continue to be fragments of community within the village in the form of a Drama Group, a Gardening Club, a Women's Institute, Bell Ringers and Sports Clubs. The church and chapel struggle on, representing a less popular God, while a huge unsightly garage seems to be a temple built for the glorification and adulation of the oil economy and the God of internal combustion. If you know the right people you can still eat pigeon pie rather than pasta, and sip bramble whisky instead of 'spring water' from a plastic bottle. In late summer too there are wild blackberries to be eaten from the hedgerow – not yet outlawed as a health risk by a European Directive.

More importantly, in some of the fields around the village, life is returning and the *culture* has been put back into *agriculture*. My concern for the lost wildlife of farming and the lost vision of the farmer led me to talk at length to two friends. I had met Gordon Beningfield, the artist and conservationist, and Sir Laurens van der Post, the writer and philosopher, through my pen. We worried for the wildlife of the general countryside and as the Royal Society for the Protection of Birds and the Wildlife Trusts were not interested at the time, we decided to go ahead with the launch of The Countryside Restoration Trust in 1993. Since that memorable day, both Gordon and Laurens have caused me to wear my funeral shoes yet again.

The aim of the CRT was to buy land that had been over-intensively farmed and to farm it in a more sensitive way, to produce quality food, wildlife and attractive landscapes. In addition, because of the great exodus from the land, we have wanted to keep the farmer and the farmworker and even put *people* back onto the land.

It has been a remarkable story. From 20 acres by the side of the brook, nearly 400 acres have become available to create Lark Rise Farm with the bulk of the land being in the village. Fields owned since 1342 have been sold to the CRT by colleges of Cambridge University – with one block of Lark Rise now amounting to nearly 300 acres, and we have almost one and half miles of brook. With land becoming available next to land already owned – Laurens van der Post would have called it 'synchronicity'.

Lark Rise has been a revelation. We have replanted its flood plains with traditional grassland, we have introduced new rotations which have broken up the old cereal monoculture. Grass margins, beetle banks, new hedges, hay meadows and a Millennium Wood have all been created and our tenant farmer – Tenant Tim – pays a lower rent than normal to compensate him for lost production – and he smiles. Stubble burning has also been banned – which makes his smile even brighter.

But what 'lost production' – for in addition to good crops, Lark Rise Farm now 'produces' wildlife – what was lost, has returned – all but the breeding lapwings. The brown hare is back to its 1950's population, there are otters in the brook, frogs in the ponds, corn buntings and English partridges in the fields, and cowslips and bee orchids in the meadows. Three years ago, barn owls successfully bred after a gap of more than forty years, and lark song again fills the summer sky: we have possibly the highest density of skylarks in East Anglia. No longer is my little farm an isolated island of farming

sanity – now it has been joined by Lark Rise and the farm of a neighbour who has just turned 'organic'. Even a pair of swallows returned to my barn in 2003 – only another thirteen pairs to go.

But there is more – in the few weak stands of scrubby elm – surviving – just – from repeated attacks of Dutch Elm Disease – we have found a butterfly – a beautiful, exquisite, fragile, secretive butterfly – the White-letter Hairstreak. Its unobtrusive caterpillar depends on the buds and leaves of elm and the butterfly briefly comes down from the foliage to feed from the flowers of bramble, thistle and privet in late July and early August. It is a remarkable appearance or reappearance – as its presence has almost certainly been permanent, and its fleeting beauty has simply been overlooked until now.

What Lark Rise has achieved has been a revelation and a transformation and shows just how quickly the land can be restored if given the chance. I believe that with sensible, honest planning, the long-term life of villages and rural communities could also be 'restored', as well as the land around them. Alas, for this to happen there has to be both the political understanding of the problems and the political will to reverse them. Politicians must realise that their policies should contain more than economics. They should be concerned about the air we breathe, the water we drink, the soil that grows our food and the communities in which we live – as well as the flow of money.

Sadly, just like my village, I too have changed during the past thirty years. I once believed in the decency of people, including politicians, and I had faith in our system of democracy. Regrettably, I now have no faith in our self-serving, manipulating politicians or the so-called and deeply flawed 'democratic process', which has so clearly failed the countryside.

I am told by those who want to 'improve' me, and direct me, that my standard of living has increased in the last thirty years – I have the benefit of new roads, runways, street lights, wheelie-bins, health centres, houses and cars, as well as access to more gadgets and electronic wonders than apples on a tree. But ironically, as my 'standard of living' has increased so the *quality of my life* has dramatically decreased because of noise pollution, light pollution, air pollution, traffic jams, no policemen, the disappearance of the family doctor, litter, agitation, regulation, speeding lorries, junk food, supermarkets,

dumbed-down television, political correctness, mindless development, materialism out of control and a number of career politicians
who clearly have never done a proper day's work in their lives.
Standard of living? I prefer *quality of life* – real stars to street lights
and the lights of Stansted airport and the gloss of short-term political
fantasies.

In thirty years, what I have seen is a growing rural tragedy:
farming systematically and cynically industrialised, village communities destroyed and country traditions attacked. These changes I have
seen from my small English village. In 1974, I wrote the first edition
of *The Decline of an English Village*. In 2004, I am watching the slow
death not just of village life, but of the whole traditional countryside
– it is the cultural cleansing of rural Britain.

The Countryside Restoration Trust

From its launch in 1993 with no land, no members and no money, the CRT has grown. It now has nearly 1,000 acres consisting not only of Lark Rise Farm in Cambridgeshire, but also Awnwells and Turnastone Court Farms in Herefordshire. In addition it has woods in Yorkshire and Essex – fields in Sussex, Norfolk and Lincolnshire, as well as the promise of more land in Surrey and Hampshire.

As a result the message of restoring the countryside, and of the good life, is spreading, as is the skylark, which has become our logo.

From those early days we now have nearly 6,000 members and we have raised in the region of £2.5 million – all without knowing how to run a charity or raise money. It has been an exciting time and a steep learning curve – a white-knuckle ride through the obstacles of 'progress', 'development', 'efficiency' and 'political correctness'. Through our commitments we also have a large bank overdraft, but we have still more costly and exciting dreams that we want to turn into reality. For those who want to join us in our efforts to restore a living, working countryside for farming, wildlife and people, please write for more details to:

The Countryside Restoration Trust,
Barton, Cambs CB3 7AG